The Collector's Encyclopedia of

R.S. PRUSSIA
and other
R.S. and E.S. Porcelain
Second Series

The Collector's Encyclopedia of

R.S. PRUSSIA
and other
R.S. and E.S. Porcelain
Second Series

by
Mary Frank Gaston

COLLECTOR BOOKS

A Division of Schroeder Publishing Co., Inc.

The current values in this book should be used only as a guide. They are not intended to set prices, which vary from one section of the country to another. Auction prices as well as dealer prices vary greatly and are affected by condition as well as demand. Neither the Author nor the Publisher assumes responsibility for any losses that might be incurred as a result of consulting this guide.

Searching For A Publisher?

We are always looking for knowledgeable people considered to be experts within their fields. If you feel that there is a real need for a book on your collectible subject and have a large comprehensive collection, contact us.

COLLECTOR BOOKS
P.O. Box 3009
Paducah, Kentucky 42002-3009

Printed by IMAGE GRAPHICS, INC., Paducah, Kentucky

Preface

Since my first book on R.S. Prussia *(The Collector's Encyclopedia of R.S. Prussia,* 1982, Collector Books, Paducah, Kentucky) was released, I have received hundreds of letters from dealers and collectors telling me how much they have enjoyed the book. I have been very pleased that the book was so well received. For the past year, I have constantly been asked when another edition was coming out. I am happy to be able to say it is now ready!

I must say that I cannot tell just how many "series" would be necessary to completely show all of the different molds, decorations, and variations thereof which were manufactured by the Schlegelmilch factories. It is important, however, not only for today's collectors, but also for future collectors, to have books which can document as many examples as possible.

In this second series, I have tried to show entirely different pieces from those in Book One. By different, I mean that not exactly the same piece with the same decoration appears in Book Two. I do, of course, show the same types of objects as well as many of the same molds and decorations and finishes. But new pieces are shown for some molds, and the same molds are shown with different decorations. For example, a bowl in the Medallion Mold is shown with a decoration different from examples featured for that Mold in my first book. Whereas only flat objects such as a bowl and a tray were shown in the Plume Mold previously, a tankard has been included in this edition.

Many new molds are also shown. The Mold Identification System has been continued, and various categories have been expanded. Although a few popular names can be applied to some molds, many do not easily lend themselves to only one identifying name. My numbering system is now used by many collectors and dealers to quickly describe various molds.

Many examples of Unmarked Prussia were featured in my first book. It is a well established fact that large amounts of R.S. Prussia were exported which were not marked. When a marked example matches an unmarked one, there is certainly no question that the pieces came from the same factory. Other pieces may have some of the same characteristics but not be identical to marked molds and decorations. The more details which match distinctive R.S. Prussia characteristics, the more probable that the piece was made by the same factory. Some of the unmarked pieces shown in my first book have now been matched to marked examples. In some cases, the marked pieces had "Steeple" or other Schlegelmilch marks rather than the R.S. Prussia mark. That information is included in the captions of the photographs. Other unmarked china has also

been included in this second book. Perhaps some of these can be clearly documented as well in the future.

Several new marks for both Erdmann and Reinhold Schlegelmilch are shown: marks previously attributed to the Schlegelmilchs which were not shown in the first book due to lack of any pieces with those marks; and some other marks not previously attributed to the Schlegelmilchs at the time I was preparing the manuscript. A few marks also are shown which have not been published in other Schlegelmilch references.

My Suggested Chronology for Schlegelmilch Marks has been revised. The revision takes into account the marks which did not appear in my earlier book. New information and material from German references has also helped to place the many marks into more limited time periods. Because some of the new material conflicts with earlier information about the factories, a detailed examination of the marks and that new material is presented.

The photograph section featuring examples of china with Schlegelmilch marks other than the R.S. Prussia mark (ES Germany, RS Suhl, RS Germany, etc.) has been greatly expanded. Items bearing some of those other marks have often been overlooked in the past. They are now beginning to come into their own. Many of those pieces appear to be really on the frontier of collectible china. I think collectors will be surprised especially to see the array of richly decorated porcelain identified with several of the ES marks.

For the readers' convenience, the Mold Identification Chart and the Marks (including the fake and misleading marks) from my first book have been reprinted in this series. Readers are referred to the earlier edition, however, for elaboration on the history of the companies, distinguishing characteristics of the porcelain, and collector's problems.

Some examples of china made and decorated by Oscar Schlegelmilch, a nephew of Erdmann and Reinhold, are shown in the last section of photographs. Oscar's factory operated during part of the same time period as his uncles'. Availability of OS china is quite limited, but the porcelain has its own special atttraction. It certainly merits collecting as part of the extended Schlegelmilch family.

Price ranges for all items featured are listed in the Value Guide at the end of the book. Prices have also been coded according to rarity, popularity, and scarcity of decoration, mold, object, and mark.

I hope you enjoy my second work on Schlegelmilch china. Hopefully this book will help partially satiate collectors' non-ceasing appetite for seeing more and more "Prussia," but I look forward to bringing you another "glimpse" of this beautiful china at some time in the future.

Mary Frank Gaston
P.O. Box 342
Bryan, Texas 77806

Readers wishing to correspond, please include a self-addressed stamped envelope. When refering to photographs in this book, use "G2" before the photograph number to avoid confusion with the photographs in my first book (G1).

Acknowledgements

Many people contributed to this book, and I sincerely appreciate the efforts of all involved. I especially thank my publisher, Bill Schroeder, Collector Books, for offering me the opportunity to write a second series on R.S. Prussia and for once again printing all of the photographs in color. The book just would not be the same without color!

I thank my editor, Steve Quertermous and his staff, for all the excellent work accomplished in producing a book. Steve always tries to have the finished product as close to my requests as possible.

I thank Mr. Ludwig Danckert, Germany, for replying to my inquiries concerning the Schlegelmilch factories. I thank Dr. Bettina Huber, Washington, D.C., for her translation of his letter.

I thank my husband, Jerry, for all his continuing help, not only for photographs, but for all the many other tasks he does to help me finish a project. The work would not go as quickly and smoothly, or be as enjoyable, without his expertise and enthusiasm!

I thank my son, Jeremy, for bearing with my time-consuming preoccupation with "china." He, too, is thrilled to see a "new" book when it comes out. His computer capabilities are put to use too whenever possible, and I imagine he will take on more in this line to help me in the future.

It is, however, with no false sincerity that I say this particular book would literally not have been possible without the help of a great many other people. Although Jerry photographed many examples, the majority of pictures were furnished by collectors across the United States and even across the waters!

From the many letters I received after my first book was released, I realized that to show as many different examples of Schlegelmilch china as possible in a second edition, I would need to visit many scattered collections. Neither time nor money would allow this, although had they been available, I would have thoroughly enjoyed meeting the challenge.

To do the next best thing, I wrote to many of the collectors who had written to me telling about their Prussia collections. I asked if they would be able to obtain photographs of pieces which could be published for another book. The response was just incredible. I received hundreds and hundreds of photographs. My hardest work was *choosing* which examples to include. Just so many pictures can be printed in a book and at the same time keep the price affordable. I had to narrow down the photographs to the 674 presented here, but that is still about one hundred more than were shown in my first book.

In addition to providing pictures, contributors supplied the pertinent information about each photographed object such as size, background color, finish and mark. Several took the time to send photographs of marks or variations of marks not shown in my first book. Their efforts involved not only time, patience and expense, but also a lot of love for this special china.

As just a small token of my appreciation to all contributors, it is my privilege and pleasure to dedicate *R.S. Prussia II* to those individuals.

To the following who really made it possible:
Richard Anderson, Beloit, Kansas
Antique Showcase, Fredricksburg, Texas
Mr. and Mrs. Robert Arbuckle
Ron Baldwin and Maxine Baldwin, Cobweb Corner Antiques, Doniphan, Nebraska
Betty and Les Bedore
Robert L. Butikas, Westville, Illinois
William A. Butikas, Westville, Illinois
Nancy and Paul Cels, Te Puke, New Zealand
Leonard "Dutch" Chevalier, Memphis, Tennessee
Nancy Clifford, Washington
Rita and Carl Clemons, Mesquite, Texas
Mrs. John D. Connell, Dallas, Texas
Mrs. Ralph Dickey, Mt. Vernon, Indiana
Elaine Dopp
Gene Galloway, The Partnership, Dallas, Texas
Robert Gollmar, Wisconsin Dells, Wisconsin
Ken Harmon
Gene Harris Auctions, Marshalltown, Iowa
Claire Hohnstein
Dee and Maurice Hooks, Lawrenceville, Illinois
Maurice L. Hooks, Washington
Mr. and Mrs. L. Edward Huber, Bethlehem, Pennsylvania
Mrs. Lyman Jeffries
Mrs. Phoebe John, Auckland, New Zealand
Robert V. Larsen Collection
John and Anna Lowe, Sharpsburg, Maryland
Mrs. J.C. McKelvain, Dallas, Texas
Emma McLean
Clarence and Ida Louise Meyer, Fort Scott, Kansas
Ruth Ann Minderman
Mel Mitchell, The Partnership, Dallas, Texas
Barbara Montgomery
Bill Moss, Memphis, Tennessee
Marti Owens
Dee Reed, Ohio
Henry G. and Edna M. Reed, Ft. Worth, Texas
Don and Irene Reeves, Fairmount, Indiana
Edward S. Rutowski, Erie, Pennsylvania
Ralph and Eunice Schlegelmilch, Lancaster, Pennsylvania
Virginia Schofner, Clearwater, Florida
T. Schwalbach, Wisconsin
Donna Smith, Yreka, California
Mrs. George Stever, Sunnyvale, California
Edward and Pamela Wolfe
Woody Auctions, Douglass, Kansas

Contents

1. New and Revised Historical Information   8

2. R.S. Prussia Mold Identification Chart   14

3. Suggested Chronology (Revised) of Schlegelmilch Marks   16

4. Marks Reprinted from 1st Edition   17

5. Additional Schlegelmilch Marks   21

6. Fake and Misleading Marks   24

7. R.S. Prussia Molds and Photographs   25

    Flat Objects   25

    Vertical Objects   84

    Accessory Items   126

    Ferners and Vases   135

8. Erdmann Schlegelmilch Porcelain: E.S. Marks   146

9. Reinhold Schlegelmilch Porcelain: other R.S. Marks   179

10. Oscar Schlegelmilch Porcelain: O.S. Marks   212

Bibliography   217

Indexes   219

    Object Index   219

    Index and Cross Reference to Popular Named Molds   220

    Decoration Themes: R.S. Prussia   221

    Decoration Themes: other Schlegelmilch Porcelain   222

Value guide to Photographs   223

1. New and Revised Historical Information

When I was preparing my first book on Schlegelmilch porcelain (*The Collector's Encyclopedia of R.S. Prussia and R.S. and E.S. Porcelain,* 1982), the only documented dates about the companies were when they were founded: Erdmann Schlegelmilch's porcelain factory was established in Suhl, Thuringia, in 1861; and Reinhold Schlegelmilch's china factory was founded in Tillowitz, Silesia, in 1869. The two brothers' factories were both located in the Germanic region generally known as "Prussia" prior to World War I. A number of marks were attributed to each factory, the most famous and coveted among American collectors being the "red" R.S. Prussia Wreath and Star Mark.

Because other books on, or containing information about, the Schlegelmilchs had not attempted to date or order chronologically any of the marks used by the two factories, I attempted to do so. I developed a possible chronology for the marks (see my first book, page 32) after several steps: (1) examining the china and noting the abundance or shortage of examples with the various marks; (2) studying the 19th century European china export trade; (3) comparing the popular art styles of the era; and (4) searching for early catalog advertisements for china.

While my book was in press, two references by German authors became available which presented new marks and some additional information about the factories. After my book was released, readers also sent some interesting and new information, including examples with marks which were not in my first book. Some of the new material by the German authors is contrary to earlier published statements and opinions about Schlegelmilch china.

Collectors should be as informed as possible about the china they collect. They should be aware of any new marks or information. If the new knowledge is in conflict with the old, the new material should be examined closely to determine what it means and how it affects our prior notions.

Who Really Used the R.S. Prussia Mark?

Schlegelmilch marks appearing in Ludwig Danckert's 1978 revised edition of his 1954 *Handbuch des Europäischen Porzellans* were sent to me in 1981 by a friend visiting Germany. (I did not have access to this new German edition at the Library of Congress while completing my original research.) By the time the material reached me, my book was already being printed.

The only major revision for Schlegelmilch marks in Danckert's 1978 book, however, is that the R.S. Prussia mark is shown only for Reinhold's factory. In his 1954 edition, the reverse had been the case! The R.S. Prussia mark was listed only for Erdmann's factory in Suhl.

According to Clifford Schlegelmilch (*Handbook of Erdmann and Reinhold Schlegelmilch,* 1973) both Erdmann and Reinhold used the R.S. Prussia mark. The author noted that the initial "R" did not stand for "Reinhold," but signified the brothers' father, "Rudolph." Because Danckert has not only continued to attribute the R.S. Prussia mark to just one Schlegelmilch factory, but has, in fact, taken the mark away from Erdmann and given it to Reinhold, I wrote Mr. Danckert for an explanation. He replied quite promptly, but the answers to my questions were not as complete as I would have liked.

Danckert informed me that the monograms used by the Schlegelmilchs were listed in a ceramic directory in 1913. He noted that the operations in Suhl at first were confined only to decorating porcelain. He also said that several Tillowitz marks were shown in the 1913 directory. Those marks had been registered in Suhl. Danckert indicated that Suhl was the "parent" house for Reinhold's Tillowitz factory.

Responding about whether Erdmann's factory also used the R.S. Prussia Wreath mark, he replied that the "Kranz" (wreath) mark with "Erdmann" printed on the left and "Reinhold" printed on the right was used by both factories. I have never seen that particular mark on a piece of china! That mark, however, does appear as Mark #16 in Schlegelmilch's book. Schlegelmilch apparently only meant to indicate that both Erdmann and Reinhold used the R.S. Prussia Wreath mark; from the manner in which the mark is printed in his book, some have erroneously inferred that there was actually such a printed mark.

In 1981, *Marks on German, Bohemian and Austrian Porcelain: 1710 to the Present* by Robert E. Röntgen was published. In that volume, several marks are shown for both Erdmann's and Reinhold's factories. The author indicates that Reinhold had both a porcelain factory and a decorating studio in Suhl and a "branch" factory in Tillowitz. That information squares with Danckert's statement that Suhl was the parent house for Reinhold's Tillowitz factory, and that Tillowitz marks were registered in Suhl. Clifford Schlegelmilch (1973) also wrote that two factories were located in Suhl, but he implied that both were operated by Erdmann. In fact, however, it appears that each brother had a factory in Suhl.

Röntgen, as Danckert, also shows the R.S. Prussia wreath mark with "Erdmann" printed on the left and "Reinhold" printed on the right. The mark is exactly the same as the one in Schlegelmilch's book. Although Danckert does not show that mark in either edition of his book, it is the one he wrote me as being used by both factories.

Röntgen indicates that the mark was an "anniversary" mark used in 1911. I assume this would have been a fifty-year anniversary, commemorating the founding of Erdmann's factory in Suhl in 1861. On page 485, however, Röntgen shows 1881 as the beginning date for Erdmann's factory. That is surely just a typographical error, because he then shows one mark for Erdmann's factory as being used "after 1861." The "anniversary" mark is also the only R.S. Prussia mark Röntgen lists for Erdmann's factory.

To my knowledge, the "anniversary" mark has not been seen on any examples of R.S. Prussia. Apparently the German authors have misinterpreted the mark from Schlegelmilch's book. If the mark is *bona fide,*

the mark must have had only limited distribution in Germany and was not used on china exported to this country!

Röntgen (as Danckert does) shows all R.S. marks to have been used only by Reinhold. The R.S. Suhl mark is also included under Reinhold's name which is contrary to Schlegelmilchs' attribution. Danckert does not illustrate the R.S. Suhl mark at all. Röntgen indicates that the R.S. Suhl mark ended in 1932. That year coincides with the time he says Reinhold's company moved to Tillowitz. When he says that Reinhold moved his factory to Tillowitz in 1932, that is confusing (see Röntgen, p. 489), because a mark from "after 1869" is shown by Röntgen to have been used by Reinhold at Tillowitz. The correct interpretation of his statement is that the main factory in Suhl closed in 1932, but the one in Tillowitz remained open—it did not just begin in 1932.

Based on both Danckert's and Röntgen's material, I think that it is logical to assume that all R.S. marks were used only by Reinhold. Because Reinhold had factories in both Suhl and Tillowitz, it is probable that the R.S. Prussia Wreath mark was used at both places. It is also possible that the factory in Tillowitz merely supplied blanks for the Suhl decorating studio with the R.S. Prussia mark affixed during the decorating process. The R.S. Suhl mark, however, logically would have been used only in Suhl.

Catalog advertisements from the late 1800s through the early 1900s refer to "Schlegelmilch," "R.S." trade marks, and "Reinhold Schlegelmilch." They do not mention "E.S." marks or "Erdmann Schlegelmilch." Because so few examples of E.S. marked china are found in comparison with R.S. marked pieces, it is reasonable to assume either that Erdmann's production was not aimed primarily at the American export trade or that his production was not as prolific as Reinhold's, or both.

In his letter to me, Danckert points out that in the 1913 directory, Reinhold's factory was shown to have employed 600 workers, whereas in the same directory, Erdmann's factory employed only 360 workers. Thus, it is apparent that Erdmann's factory was smaller than Reinhold's. Reinhold was noted in the same directory to have manufactured "luxury" porcelain, vases, and children's dishes. He was also listed as having a "sample" factory (probably showroom) in New York. Erdmann was shown as supplying "special" china to the American and English markets.

Assigning Dates to Schlegelmilch Marks

Although I presented a "Suggested Chronology" for Schlegelmilch marks in my first book, I did not attempt to place any specific year date on any mark. That is, I did not say a mark began in 1875 or was used between 1865 and 1880, for example. I only suggested some general time periods for when the marks logically could have been used.

Röntgen (1981) does give year dates for all of the Schlegelmilch marks he shows. There are several problems with his dating information, however. First, many of the marks are shown to have been used during the same time period. For example, the R.S. Prussia Wreath mark, and the R.S. Germany, R.S. Tillowitz, and Royal Silesia marks are all dated between 1904 and 1938.

Second, some dates are not indicated specifically, only "after" a certain year. That method of dating is too broad. It actually means only "not before" a certain time. Dates designated as "after" are often inferred to mean "soon" after, however. If businesses were in operation for a number of years, as the Schlegelmilchs', "after 1861" or "after 1891," could actually be as late as 1930.

Third, several dates are enclosed in parentheses. According to Röntgen, dates so indicated note the first time the mark was actually seen or known to have been in use. The author does say, however, that such marks could have been in use some years earlier. For some of the Schlegelmilch marks which have such a notation (year enclosed within parentheses), I would suggest that the time shown is probably quite a few years later than when the mark was really first used.

By looking at Röntgen's marks for the Schlegelmilch factories, it is apparent that the dates he assigns to those marks and the dating periods I suggested in my first book do not dovetail. But my chronological order was basically the same as his. For example, the Steeple marks precede the R.S. Prussia and R.S. Germany marks. I have somewhat revised my chronology, however, because of now having seen actual examples with some of the marks not shown in my first book. From those specimens, as well as additional samples with some of the other ES and RS marks, it is possible not only to revise the chronology of the marks but also to narrow their probable period of use.

The revised dating periods still do not match all those shown by Röntgen. In the next section, I will focus on why I agree or disagree with his dates for Erdmann's and Reinhold's marks.

Erdmann Schlegelmilch's Marks

Danckert, Schlegelmilch, and Röntgen all show that Erdmann used many different marks on his china. Examples of all of those marks, however, are not found. I discussed those "unseen" marks in my first book. They included several "Bird" marks and two "Suhl" marks (one a crown with "Schlegelmilch 1861 Suhl" printed in a simple cartouche; and a small ellipse, topped by a bow and ribbon with "Suhl" printed in the middle).

According to Röntgen's dates, the Suhl ellipse mark was used "after 1861." One Bird mark (a bird in a dotted oval shape, topped by a bow) is dated "(1886)"; and two other Bird marks are shown to have been used about 1896. A fourth Bird mark (the only one I showed earlier, see Mark 18) is not shown with a beginning date. All of the Bird marks, however, are listed by Röntgen as having been in use until 1938.

The ES Crown mark and ES script marks were not used until after 1891, according to Röntgen. Two other ES marks which were first attributed by Dan-

ckert in his 1978 edition are: (1) "Suhl" printed within a banner with "Prussia China" printed above, and (2) a printed ES monogram mark (see Mark 41). Röntgen indicates those two marks were used "circa" 1900 and "after" 1900 respectively. The ES Royal Saxe mark as well as a Beehive mark with "Germany" printed below are listed also by Röntgen as being used "after" 1900.

Several marks known by collectors as the "Prov Sxe" marks are noted by Röntgen as beginning in 1902. The last date he gives for any of Erdmann's marks is 1938. Although Röntgen does not show a final date for all of Erdmann's marks, when a final date is noted, it appears that all of the Bird marks, the Beehive mark, ES printed monogram, and Prov Sxe marks were all used until 1938, although each was instituted at different times. That does not seem plausible.

To date, I have no information of pieces in this country with the Suhl Elipse mark, the Suhl banner mark, or the Suhl Crown mark. As I said in my earlier book, lack of examples with those marks suggests that china so marked was not exported to this country. It is logical to assume that those marks, however, were among the early marks used by Erdmann's factory.

A few examples have been located with three of the Bird marks (see Marks 18, 36, and 37). Mark 18, in fact, was shown in my first edition. The few examples found with the Bird marks also indicate that those marks were not used on exported china. The rare examples which do come on the market were probably brought to this country by German settlers. With the exception of pieces with Mark 18, the Bird marks do appear to be earlier than the familiar Schlegelmilch marks.

The shape and decoration of the examples with Bird Marks (Mark 36 and 37) reflect the naturalistic trend which became popular in Europe during the 1870s and then in America in the 1880s. A tankard (see #438) is very much in the style of the American Belleek porcelain manufactured by Ott & Brewer in Trenton, New Jersey, during the 1880s. The cracker jar (see #439) also shows intricate workmanship in the cut-out work on the sides and the tapestry body. The 1880 period would seem more logical than the 1896 date Röntgen notes the marks were first seen.

Another mark which has not been shown by other references is an ES monogram printed in a cursive style and enclosed within a circle (see Mark 35). The mark is also printed in brown like two of the Bird marks. Based on the rarity of pieces with this mark and the decoration of the example I show (see #441), the mark was probably used during the same time period, possibly even a few years earlier (1880s) than those Bird Marks.

Porcelain marked with the ES Crown or the ES Royal Saxe marks are scarce, but examples are not as rare as the Bird marks. The Crown marks may represent the beginning of Erdmann's exported production to the United States. The pieces look later than those with the Bird marks. They have artistic shapes, but the decoration is transfer and not individualized. Röntgen's dates of "after 1891" for the ES Crown mark (see Mark 23) and "after 1900" for the ES Royal Saxe Mark (see Mark 22) seem to be near the right time period, that is, circa the 1890s. An interesting decoration of Indian subjects is found on some pieces with the ES Crown and Royal Saxe marks. Undoubtedly, the manufacturer was catering to what he thought Americans would like to see!

Many examples of Erdmann's china are marked "Prov Sxe" (see Marks 19-21, 39, and 40). A large amount of that porcelain is styled along Art Nouveau lines. Although transfers continued to be used, the appeal of the sensuous shapes as well as the fanciful figures such as the "Lady with Peacock," "Lady with Doves," and "Sea Goddess" are extremely attractive. Brilliant colors, gold trim, pearlized lusters, and tapestry beading were used to enhance the porcelain. These pieces were surely made during the early 1900s until the World War I era, the same period I suggested in my earlier book. That time also agrees with the "circa 1902" date Röntgen shows for the marks.

China with Erdmann's script marks (see Mark 17), the printed SE monogram (see Mark 41), and Bird Mark (Mark #18) all look to be much later than the Prov Sxe pieces. Röntgen's date of "after 1891" for the script marks is too ambiguous, and his date of circa 1900 for the printed SE monogram seems too early. Examples with all of those marks are quite plain in shape. Those marks are found on table wares or decorative plates with floral transfer decoration.

The change from display porcelain such as vases modeled in the Art Nouveau fashion to "useful" table china, simply shaped and simply decorated, reflects the state of the European export china market after World War I. The demand for luxurious decorative porcelain became small, and the Art Nouveau style began to be replaced by a turn to simplicity and modernism. Some of the plainer pieces with Prov Sxe marks seem to show that transition.

The market for all types of china decreased greatly after the stock market crash of 1929 and the following years of the world-wide Depression. European china factories which had relied on the American trade found themselves out of business or forced to limit sharply their production. Erdmann's factory seems to have fallen victim to those circumstances. Danckert reports in his letter that Erdmann's factory employed 300 workers in 1930, but the factory closed seven years later, in 1937.

Reinhold Schlegelmilch's Marks

Danckert (1978) attributes four marks to Reinhold's Tillowitz factory which he did not show for that company in his 1954 edition. One was the R.S. Prussia Wreath mark (discussed above) which he had previously attributed to Erdmann. Another was the R.S. Poland mark. Both of those marks are, of course, familiar to U.S. collectors. Schlegelmilch (1973) shows the R.S. Poland mark for Reinhold's factory. That mark is often found in conjunction with Reinhold's blue underglaze R.S. Germany mark, further substantiating the fact that the Poland mark (see Mark 33) was used by Reinhold rather than Erdmann.

New R.S. Tillowitz Mark

In the revised 1978 edition of Danckert's book, a mark containing the initials "RST" printed vertically and enclosed within a dotted oval is shown for Reinhold's Tillowitz factory. As far as I know, that particular mark has not been found on china in this country. Röntgen dates the mark circa 1916. That date would place its use right in the middle of World War I, and thus the absence of any known examples in the United States is understandable.

New "Wing" Mark

The other new mark for Reinhold (Danckert, 1978) has been seen on a very limited amount of porcelain. The mark is rather intricate. Fancy wings are on either side of an RS monogram, and a star is at the top of the mark (see Mark 49). Röntgen shows the mark to be "after 1869" through 1938. Although the date is ambiguous, the mark may well be among the first marks Reinhold used.

We know the mark was not used on exported china because too few examples have been found. Pieces with the mark, however, are clearly decorated differently from other R.S. Prussia, R.S. Germany, R.S. Suhl, R.S. Silesia, or R.S. Poland china. The dainty floral sprays are more along the lines of decoration associated with the Haviland company in Limoges, France. The china, itself, is thin, and the shape is not as ornate as R.S. Prussia molds. The shape is not as plain as most R.S. Germany designs. The mark, printed in brown like Erdmann's Bird marks (Marks 36 and 37), would seem to indicate its comparable age.

Steeple Marks

Two other marks, coined by collectors as "Steeple" marks (see Marks 1 to 3) are also found on a limited amount of examples. The Steeple marks, however, are not as rare as the Wing mark. The Steeple marked pieces have their own unique characteristics. The shapes are rococo, the colors are deep, including cobalt blue, Tiffany bronze, and heavy gold. Floral or figural transfers are the general decoration themes.

The Steeple marks are simple in form, thereby suggesting they are earlier than the more elaborate R.S. Wreath marks, as I said in my first book. Steeple marked china is, in fact, quite similar to Erdmann's E.S. Crown and Royal Saxe marked porcelain. Röntgen shows the Steeple marks to have been used between 1898 and 1908. That time period is in the same era he gives for those ES marks (1891 and 1900). I would place the Steeple marks at an earlier time, however, circa the late 1870s or early 1880s.

It seems illogical that Reinhold did not export porcelain to America before 1898. From Röntgen's dates, however, that is what must be inferred. With the exception of the Wing mark (dated "after 1869"), the earliest date Röntgen gives for any of Reinhold's marks is the 1898 date for the Steeple marks. I noted in my first book that Reinhold probably exported porcelain before Erdmann did, and I also said that Reinhold probably did not begin exporting as soon as he established a factory. My chronology reflected that assumption.

R.S. Wreath Marks

The artistic shapes of the Steeple marked china visually seem to progress toward the unique "Prussian" style. Molds become more ornate and decoration increasingly elaborate. It would have been only fitting to change the simple Steeple marks to the fancier multicolored RSP Wreath mark to identify that distinctive production.

Röntgen tell us, however, that the R.S. Prussia Wreath mark as well as the other R.S. Wreath marks were all used during the same time period: 1904-1938. (Note that he does show that the R.S. Suhl mark ended in 1932. That date coincides with his information that Reinhold's Suhl factory closed in 1932, but the Tillowitz factory was in operation until 1938, see Röntgen, p. 489.)

There are several reasons why the RS Wreath marks would not have been used simultaneously. Recall that Röntgen notes that 1904 is the first year when the R.S. Prussia and R.S. Suhl marks were first documented. This could easily have been because of the 1904 exhibition in Leipzeig. That exhibition featured porcelain made by factories in Thuringia, the German region where Suhl was located. It is very conceivable that pieces with R.S. Prussia and R.S. Suhl marks were first recorded by German ceramic historians at that time. It certainly does not mean that either mark was first instituted by the factory in 1904. More conclusive evidence against Röntgen's 1904 date for the R.S. Prussia mark is the fact that Catalog advertisements in the late 1880s and late 1890s featured R.S. Prussia china! (See Barlock, p. 5.)

In comparison with R.S. Prussia, R.S. Suhl pieces have different shapes and decoration, and are scarce. Lines are simple and decoration is more subdued. The background colors are often dark, and transfer subjects are usually figural (often classical and allegorical subjects) rather than floral. The R.S. Suhl mark is found primarily on decorative items rather than table china. The R.S. Suhl marks seem to parallel Erdmann's Art Nouveau production and precede R.S. Germany marks which are largely found on table china and white ware. The R.S. Suhl mark may not have been intended for export ware because so few examples are found in comparison to both R.S. Prussia and R.S. Germany pieces. Undoubtedly, the R.S. Suhl mark did overlap with the R.S. Prussia mark, but I would place it no earlier than 1900.

Catalog advertisements inform us that the R.S. Germany mark was definitely being used by 1913. Some of the shapes shown for the company in that year are identical or similar to those which have R. S. Suhl marks. R.S. Germany marked china is basically completely different from R.S. Prussia. The plain lines and restrained floral decor are evidence of the changing artistic tastes of the pre-World War I years. The stylized floral designs reflect the final days of Art Nouveau, but clean lines preview the beginning of the Art Deco era.

Porcelain with R.S. Germany marks which has the same elaborate shapes or identical molds to R.S. Prussia marked pieces can be accounted for simply by the fact that most china factories continued to use some of the same molds after marks were changed.

The scarcity of R.S. Prussia molds with R.S. Germany marks proves that the practice was not continued for very long. The rococo R.S. Prussia molds were abandoned in favor of the developing taste for a "modern" simple line.

The R.S. Tillowitz, Silesia mark, and the R.S. Royal Silesia mark (see Marks 30-32) appear to have been used later than the R.S. Germany marks. Some of those pieces are definitely in the Art Deco style. Others represent tableware patterns like those manufactured by other European and American china manufacturers during the 1930s. Both of these marks are seldom seen. Another Tillowitz mark shown by Danckert, Schlegelmilch, and Röntgen is also rare. That mark is a fancy R.S. Tillowitz script mark. Röntgen notes that the mark was not used until 1932.

I have included another version of the Tillowitz Wreath mark in this book which appears to be rare as well (see Mark 50). The mark is quite different from other R.S. marks. It is composed of a large transfer stamp featuring a woman with a bow and arrow. "Diana China" is printed around the border of the mark, and the R.S. Tillowitz Wreath and Star mark are barely visible at the base of the mark. The mark was found on a dinner service having a cream colored glaze and pastel floral border design, typical 1930s decor.

The rarity of the R.S. Tillowitz and Royal Silesia marks can be accounted for by the unsettled 1930s time period. World economic conditions and the beginning of a second World War in Europe brought the European china exporting business almost to a standstill until some years after the end of World War II.

R.S. Poland Mark

Röntgen dates the Poland mark between 1919 and 1921 (see Marks 33 and 34). That time does not coincide with the 1916-1918 period some collectors consider to be correct. His dates are also contrary to the post World War II time I suggested for the mark in my first book.

Based on a Polish author's work (Leon Chroscicki, *Porcelana--Znaki Wytworni Europejskich*, 1974), and my own historical research, I could only conclude that the mark was not used before 1945. Danckert did not offer me any information about the mark except to say that Tillowitz is now a part of Poland, which I have said already in my first book. Danckert said, in his letter to me, that he did not have access to Chroscicki's 1974 book.

Chroscicki (1974) shows that Reinhold's Tillowitz factory was taken over by the Polish state circa 1956. The town had been in an area administered by Poland between the end of World War II and 1956. According to Chroscicki, Reinhold's Wreath mark, after 1956, was changed to reflect state ownership of the factory. The RS initials became PT (Poland, Tillowitz). "Made in Poland" was printed below the Wreath. "Made in" is found only in this and the R.S. Poland mark. Although there is no specific year when "Made in" was required by America (or any other country) to be part of a mark, the term was not generally used in marks until after the 1920s.

Röntgen notes the last information he has of Reinhold's factory is 1938. He does not list Chroscicki in his references, and thus, evidently, he did not know of Chroscicki's later facts about the factory. I have no reason to change my earlier conclusion about the post World War II date for the R.S. Poland mark. (See page 22 in my first book for discussion of the historical data concerning this mark.)

Other Marks Attributed to Reinhold

An interesting mark was brought to my attention last year by a collector in New Zealand. Pictures were sent to me of china marked "Friedrich II." Some of the pieces had only the Friedrich II mark while others also had the underglaze R.S. Germany mark (see Mark 53). There is no doubt that the pieces were either manufactured by the Schlegelmilch company or made from the molds of that factory. The decoration is also similar to that found on R.S. Germany (see photographs 650 to 656).

Although examples are not numerous, both the R. S. Prussia mark and the R.S. Germany mark can be found in conjunction with some other mark. In some cases, the other mark is that of a decorating firm, such as the Pickard studio. Other double marks seem to be those of exporters or importers. I believe the Friedrich II mark is probably one used by a non-American importer. See Marks 45, 46, and 48 for examples of some similar types of double marks.

Also it was not an uncommon practice for foreign importers to have their own marks put on china in place of the manufacturer's mark. One good example of this practice found on Schlegelmilch porcelain is the Wheelock Trade Mark (see Mark 51). According to Lois Lehner in her *Complete Book of American Kitchen and Dinner Ware,* 1980, the Wheelock company, established in Peoria, Illinois, in 1888, imported European china and had its own trade mark applied. Pieces with the Wheelock Prussia mark are found with identical molds and decoration of various R.S. Prussia marked pieces. The lettering of "Prussia" underneath the mark is also the same in color and style to that found in the R.S. Prussia mark. There should be no doubt that Wheelock Prussia and R.S. Prussia are one and the same!

A similar example to the Wheelock mark is another mark of a Crown with "Viersa" printed underneath (see Mark 52). I am told that mark is frequently seen in Canada. Pieces are also identical in mold and decoration to some R.S. Prussia marked china.

Oscar Schlegelmilch

According to Schlegelmilch (1973), Oscar Schlegelmilch was a nephew of Erdmann and Reinhold. Oscar manufactured porcelain in Langewiessen, a town, which like Suhl, was located in the region of Thuringia. The company was established in 1892. Röntgen states that the factory was in business until 1972 when it became a part of the VEB Porcelain Combine in Colditz.

A number of marks are attributed by Danckert and Schlegelmilch to Oscar's factory. Röntgen shows the same marks with dates. Very little of Oscar's produc-

tion appears to have been exported because examples are quite scarce. Most of the pieces shown in this book all have the same mark, the "O.S. St. Kilian, Germany" mark (see Mark 54). That particular mark is noted by Röntgen to have first been documented in 1904, the same time he shows for the R.S. Wreath marks.

Examples with the St. Kilian mark are richly decorated with classical and mythological scenes. The shapes are not as ornate as R.S. Prussia, but they are more ornate than R.S. Germany marked china. Overall, they appear to be more in the style of R.S. Suhl and E.S. Germany china.

Other marks attributed to Oscar's factory include a Beehive (see Mark 55); an OS monogram; a four-leaf Clover with the initials "OS"; a Crown and "L"; a Crown topped by a cross; and a Crown and "L" combined with Oscar's full name (see Mark 56). Röntgen's dates for most of those marks are broad or only show a beginning year. The Crown and "L" with Oscar's name is noted not to have been seen until 1950. The one example I show with that mark does appear to be post World War II. Readers are referred to Danckert, Schlegelmilch, and Röntgen (see bibliography) for examples of those other marks. I had no pieces with those marks which prevented my including them in this book.

Problems with Marks

Most of the Schlegelmilch porcelain which has another mark combined with the Schlegelmilch mark, such as the Pickard decorating mark or a department store mark, really do not present a problem for collectors. The various shades of color for the R.S. Prussia mark can be explained by variations in firing the marks, and those varying colors should not be of concern to collectors. But some other marks continue to be confusing or misleading.

Mold Marks

Embossed stars, raised circles, elongated ridges, and so forth do not by themselves identify porcelain as a piece of Schlegelmilch china. I discussed this in detail in my first book (see page 25). In that book, I printed several mold marks (see Marks 10-14). The photographs, however, have helped only to perpetuate the thought that "Mold" marks alone indicate that a piece of china is R.S. Prussia.

When "mold" marks are found in combination with a Schlegelmilch mark, the piece is, of course, a product of one of the factories. When a piece has only the "mold" mark but is identical to another piece with a printed Schlegelmilch mark, then the unmarked piece can also be attributed correctly to the Schlegelmilchs.

George W. Terrell in *Collecting R.S. Prussia, Identification and Values*, 1982, page 3, says that "The oldest ware considered to be 'Prussia' produced by a Schlegelmilch firm is either unmarked or marked only with some type of raised designs." Terrell is correct when he says "considered" to be the oldest, but there is no consensus about any evidence to substantiate that as factual.

Beehive Marks

Several references attribute a Beehive mark to Erd-

mann's factory. Röntgen shows a Beehive with "Germany" printed beneath the mark to have been used by Erdmann's factory. Sometimes a Beehive mark is found alongside an R.S. Wreath mark (see Mark 16), and one of the Prov Sxe marks does incorporate a Beehive as part of the mark (see Mark 40).

According to Danckert, and as I said in my first book, many companies used a Beehive mark in an effort to mislead people into thinking that the china was a product of the Royal Vienna factory. The presence of a Beehive mark by itself cannot be used to identify Schlegelmilch china.

Fake and Misleading Marks

Regrettably, fake R.S. Prussia marks are still around (see Mark R1). The "misleading" marks are also just as prevalent as they were several years ago (see Marks R2-R4). The high prices realized for authentic R.S. Prussia make such practices profitable it seems. In this edition, I have also included a hand-painted fake RSP mark (see Mark R5). That particular mark was underglaze. At a distance it did look genuine. Remember to examine all RSP marks carefully. They are overglaze marks. They are not underglaze like the blue R.S. Germany mark. The RSP mark should show some wear and not be perfect!

Because china painting has once again become a popular hobby, do not be surprised to see RSP subjects on new china. I have been amazed with the orders I have received from china painters for my first R.S. Prussia book. Just remember, authentic pieces do not have totally handpainted decoration.

I have also seen new ceramic work in shapes similar to RSP molds. The pieces have transfer decoration such as the Melon Eaters and Countess Potocka. The items also had a fake RSP mark. The obvious clue that the objects are not genuine is the fact that they are earthenware and not porcelain. Be sure pieces are translucent and not opaque! (Some earthenware, non-translucent china, was made by the Schlegelmilchs, but such pieces are seldom seen.) Remember 99.9% of all Schlegelmilch china is true porcelain!

It is difficult to keep up with faked molds and hand-painted decoration made by various individuals. Collectors just must always be on the alert for pieces that "don't look right." On the other hand, most advanced collectors are aware of the several items of new china which are currently being sold through wholesale centers to antique dealers, gift shops, and other commercial outlets. Several of those items are made in shapes similar to, or identical with, genuine R.S. Prussia molds. Several of those items were shown in my earlier book (see pages 210-212). Those pieces frequently have one of the "misleading" printed marks, or sometimes the purchaser places one of the "fake" decal RSP marks on the object. The same pieces of china may also be found with "Limoges" or "Nippon" printed marks. Since those names are generic, they do not violate any specific company trade mark, and thus the manufacturers take advantage of those highly "collectible" names. The decoration on the new china is not identical to RSP themes, but it is often similar. I have listed molds which are currently being copied in the captions of the photographs of the authentic molds.

2. R.S. Prussia Mold Identification Chart

Category 1—Flat or Round Objects

Mold Numbers*	Photo Numbers	Type of Mold	General Characteristics
1-50	1-70	Popular Named Molds (Iris, etc.)	A particular feature in the body or the border of the mold suggests an obvious mold name.
51-75	71-75	Floral Border Molds	The border of the mold is composed of floral designs usually separated by other shapes such as scallops or points. The floral designs are not always easy to see at first glance.
76-150	76-106	Unusual Body Shape	The body of the mold is composed of blown out sections usually in the form of dome or star shapes.
151-180	107-110	Pointed Border Molds	The overall border design is pointed. There may be notched indentations between the points. Such molds must be easily distinguishable from scalloped molds and have no rounded sides.
181-200	111-115	Rounded Scalloped Border	Border has rounded scallop sections of equal size. The sections may be beaded or fluted.
201-250	116-129	Semi-Round Scalloped Border	The scallop sections are not perfectly round. There may be a slight indentation or some other configuration between the scallops. The edges of the scallops can be smooth, beaded, or fluted.
251-275	130-141	Crimped Scalloped Border	Scallop sections are pinched or indented.
276-299	142-145	Wavy Scalloped Border	The scallop sections resemble a wavy line with a slight rounded center and shallow indentations on each side. The wavy sections may be separated by other small configurations such as scroll designs or points.
300-325	146-163	Elongated Scalloped Border	The scallop sections are long rather than round. The center of the section has either a slight indentation, or a sharp rounded point. The elongated scallops may be separated by other small configurations.
326-400	164-185	Irregular Scalloped Borders	Borders are composed of more than one of the above kind of scallops or some other configuration such as a point or scroll design. These molds are usually quite elaborate.
401-425	186,187	Scrolled Borders	Border is composed of ornate, curving scallop designs not only on the border but extending into the body of the object.
426-450	188,189	Smooth Borders	Border is completely smooth. The overall shape of the object may vary: round, oval, or rectangular.

*Please note that some examples of RSP Molds shown in my first book are not repeated in this book. Those Molds and their numbers can be found in that first edition. Some new molds, which are very similar to, but not identical with, other molds have been assigned mold numbers with "a, b, c" added to the number. Some new molds are described briefly in their first caption to point out distinguishing characteristics which may not be obvious in the photograph.

Mold numbers in Category 3--Accessories have been changed slightly to include a few additional types of items.

Category 2—Vertical or Tall Objects

Mold Numbers*	Photo Numbers	Type of Mold	General Characteristics
451-500	190-209	Smooth Bases	Base of object is perfectly level or flat on the bottom.
501-575	210-290	Flat Scalloped Base	The border of the base of the object is scalloped, but there is no elevation.
576-600	291-303	Elevated Scalloped Base	The base of the object has a scalloped border composed of equal or varied sized scallops. Indentations between the scallops elevate the object slightly.
601-625	304-317	Pedestal Foot	Objects may have a long or a short pedestal base. Long pedestals have a stem section between the base and body; short pedestals have no stem section. The bases of the pedestals may be round, square, smooth, or scalloped.
626-700	318-364	Molded Feet	Feet for the object are shaped as part of the body mold.
701-725	365-367	Applied Feet	Definite feet are applied to the base of the object.

Category 3—Accessory Items

Mold Numbers*	Photo Numbers	Type of Mold	
726-775	368-378	Hatpin Holders	
776-800	379-382	Muffineers/Talcum Shakers	
801-825	383-386	Hair Receivers	
826-850	387-392	Pin Boxes/Powder Boxes	
851-855	393	Candle Holders	
856-860	394	Letter Holders	
861-875	395-399	Shaving Mugs	

Category 4—Ferners and Vases

Mold Numbers*	Photo Numbers	Type of Mold	
876-899	400-403	Ferners	
900-950	404-437	Vases	

3. Suggested Chronology (Revised) of R.S. and E.S. Schlegelmilch Marks

Erdmann Schlegelmilch (porcelain factory established in Suhl, Prussia, circa 1869 closed circa 1937).

Marks 35-37	E.S. Script Monogram and Bird Marks	circa 1880s
Marks 22, 23, 38	E.S. Crown and E.S. Royal Saxe Marks	circa 1890s
Marks 19-21, 39, 40	Prov Sxe Marks	circa 1900 to 1920
Marks 17, 18, 41	E.S. Script; Crown and Bird; and printed Monogram Marks	circa 1920s to 1930s

Reinhold Schlegelmilch (porcelain factories established in Suhl, Prussia, and Tillowitz, Silesia, circa 1869; Suhl factory closed circa 1932 (Röntgen, 1981); Tillowitz factory under administration of Poland after 1945 to 1956; factory taken over by the state (Poland) circa 1956 (Chroscicki, 1974).

Mark 49	Wing Mark	possibly used during the 1870s; too few examples available for definite conclusion
Marks 1-3, 42	Steeple Marks	circa 1870s to 1880s
Marks 4-11, 15, 43-46, 51, 52	R.S. Prussia Wreath Marks and Exporter Marks	circa mid-1880s to 1910
Marks 16, 47	R.S. Suhl Marks	circa early 1900s
Marks 24-29, 48, 53	R.S. Germany Marks and Exporter Marks	circa 1910 to 1956
Marks 30-32	R.S. Tillowitz; R.S. Silesia Marks	circa early 1930s to 1940s
Marks 33, 34	R.S. Poland Marks	circa 1945 to 1956

4. Marks Reprinted from 1st Edition

MARK 1. red, Tillowitz.

MARK 2. dark green, Tillowitz.

MARK 3. red, Tillowitz.

MARK 4. red, Suhl or Tillowitz.

MARK 5. green, Suhl or Tillowitz.

MARK 6. red with gold "Handpainted," Suhl or Tillowitz.

MARK 7. green RSP with red RSG, Tillowitz.

MARK 8. red RSP, red RSG, Tillowitz.

MARK 9. red RSP, gold RSG, Tillowitz.

MARK 10. red RSP, Suhl or Tillowitz, with mold mark.

MARK 11. red RSP, Suhl or Tillowitz, with mold mark.

MARK 12. mold mark, origin undetermined.

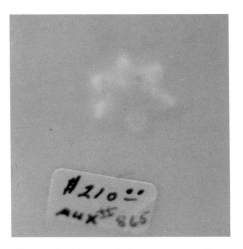

MARK 13. mold mark, origin undetermined.

MARK 14. mold mark, origin undetermined.

MARK 15. red RSP, Suhl or Tillowitz, with **gold** Royal Vienna Mark.

MARK 16. red (or green not pictured), Suhl, with or without blue beehive.

MARK 17. red Suhl.

MARK 18. blue-green, Suhl.

MARK 19. green, Suhl.

MARK 20. green, Suhl.

MARK 21. green, Suhl.

MARK 22. green, Suhl.

MARK 23. green, Suhl.

MARK 24. blue RSG with red script, Tillowitz.

MARK 25. blue RSG, Tillowitz.

MARK 26. green RSG, Tillowitz.

MARK 27. green RSG, Tillowitz.

MARK 28. green RSG (with or without "Handpainted"), Tillowitz.

MARK 29. gold "Hand-painted" RSG, Tillowitz.

MARK 30. blue R. S. Tillowitz (with or without Silesia, Germany, or "Handpainted"), Tillowitz.

MARK 31. green or blue R.S. Silesia, Tillowitz.

MARK 32. uncolored R.S. Silesia, Tillowitz.

MARK 33. red R.S. Poland with blue RSG and gold "Handpainted," Tillowitz.

MARK 34. red R.S. Poland (with or without "Germany" or "Hand-painted"), Tillowitz.

5. Additional Schlegelmilch Marks

MARK 35. brown ES Script Monogram, Suhl.

MARK 36. brown ES Bird, Suhl.

MARK 37. brown ES Bird, Suhla, Suhl.

MARK 38. green numbers similar to ES Mark 23 with gold "Royal Windsor," Germany.

MARK 39. green, Suhl.

MARK 40. green, Suhl.

MARK 41. green ES Printed Monogram, Suhl.

MARK 42. gold RS Steeple Mark, Tillowitz.

MARK 43. red RSP, gold "Gesetzlich Geschutzt" (patent mark).

MARK 44. red RSP with mold mark.

MARK 45. red RSP with gold "BT Co" mark.

MARK 46. red RSP with gold "Dresden" mark.

MARK 47. green RS Suhl mark, Suhl.

MARK 48. green RSG with green "BT Co" mark.

MARK 49. brown RS Germany Wing mark, Tillowitz.

MARK 50. brown and turquoise RS Tillowitz mark, Tillowitz (with pattern name).

MARK 51. red and green, Wheelock Prussia, American importer, Tillowitz or Suhl.

MARK 52. red Crown "Viersa" mark, origin Suhl or Tillowitz.

MARK 53. blue RSG with gold (or green) Friedrich II, origin Suhl or Tillowitz.

MARK 54. green OS (Oscar Schlegelmilch) St. Kilian, Langewiessen, Thuringia.

MARK 55. green OS mark with Beehive, Langewiessen.

MARK 56. blue OS Crown and L mark, Langewiessen.

6. Fake and Misleading Marks

R1. Reproduced R. S. Prussia Mark.

R2. in red, initials, wreath, and star.

R3. in red, initials, wreath, and star.

R4. wreath and star.

R5. Fake handpainted R. S. Prussia Mark.

7. R.S. Prussia Molds and Photographs*
Flat Objects
Popular Named Molds (Photographs 1 to 38)

1. Mold 2a. "Grape" Mold Variation. Bowl, 10¼"d, Poppies, stencilled gold designs on inner border and in alternating reserves.

2. Mold 2b. "Grape" Mold Variation. Berry Bowl, 10½"d.

3. Mold 2c. "Grape" Mold Variation. Bowl, 11½"d.

*All pieces shown in this section are marked RSP unless otherwise indicated.

25

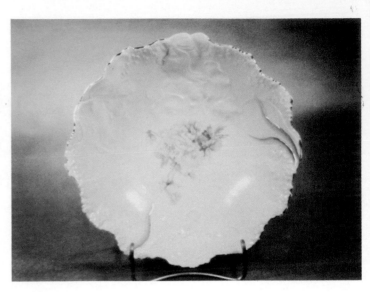

4. Mold 4. "Hidden Image" Mold. One example in this mold has been reported with "Germany Saxe, Altenburg" as the mark. Altenburg, like Suhl was also in Thuringia. The mark has not been documented and could refer to a decorating studio. Note that all pieces with the Hidden Images have the same Mold Number although the images are not exactly alike. Bowl, 10¼"d, "Hidden Lady" at top, pearl finish, unmarked.

5. Mold 4. "Hidden Image" Mold. Bowl, 7¾"d, pearl finish, unmarked.

7. Mold 4. "Hidden Image" Mold. Relish or Serving Bowl, 12"l, gold beaded border, Shadow Flowers, unmarked.

6. Mold 4. "Hidden Image" Mold. Cake Plate, 9¾"d, unmarked.

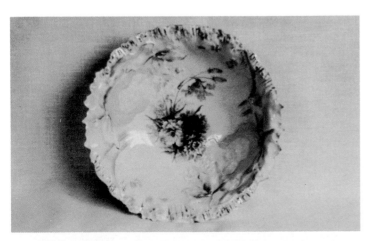

8. Mold 4. "Hidden Image" Mold. This Mold has a Double Image, one lady on each side. Bowl, 10"d, unmarked.

9. Mold 4. "Hidden Image" Mold. Double Image at top of Cake Plate, 11¾"d, unmarked.

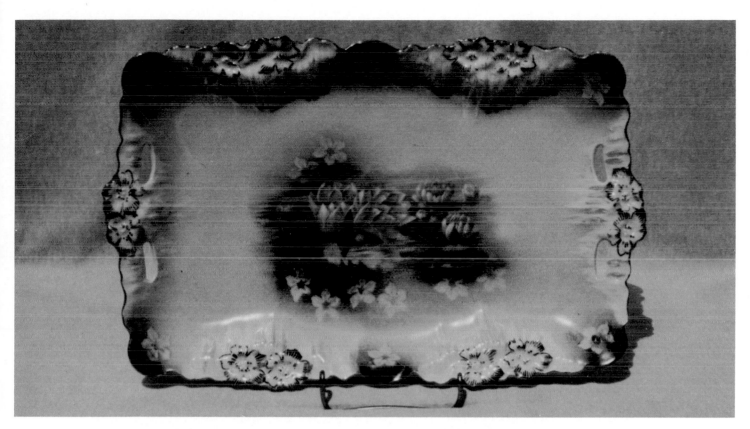

10. Mold 7. "Icicle" Mold. Tray, 11¾"x7¼", Reflecting Water Lilies, unmarked.

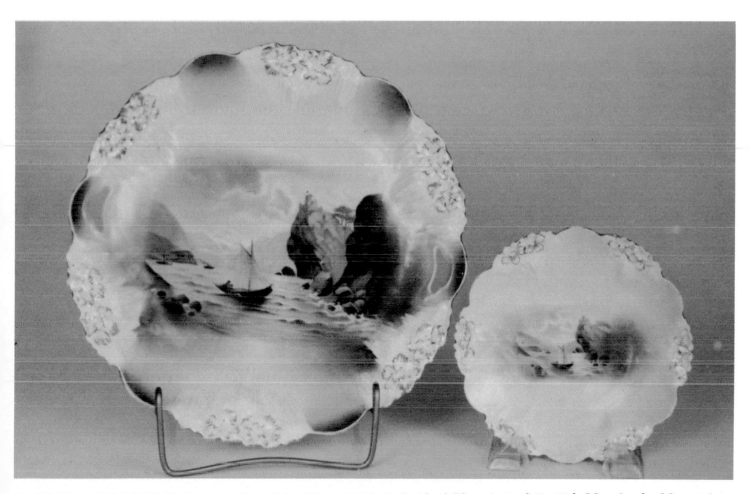

11. Mold 7. "Icicle" Mold. Dessert Set: Cake Plate, 10"d, Individual Plate (set of 6), 5"d, Man in the Mountain.

12. Mold 9. "Fleur-de-lys" Mold. Plate, 8½"d, Poppies, satin finish.

13. Mold 9. "Fleur-de-lys" Mold. Bowl, 9¼"d, Roses, unmarked.

14. Mold 10a. "Leaf" Mold Variation. Dish, 5½"l, 5½"w, Dogwood Blossoms.

15. Mold 10b. "Leaf" Mold Variation. Dish, 9"d, Tulips.

16. Mold 10c. "Leaf" Mold Variation. Cake Plate, 10"d, Poppies.

17. Mold 10d. "Leaf" Mold Variation. Dish, 8¼"d, Pink Roses, pearl finish.

18. Mold 10d. "Leaf" Mold Variation. Dish, 6½"d, Tiffany finish at base.

19. Mold 12a. "Lettuce" Mold Variation. Bowl, 9″d, Roses.

20. Mold 12b. "Lettuce" or "Cabbage" Mold Variation. Bowl, 4½″d, 2½″h, Underplate, 6½″d, Mark 15.

21. Mold 14. "Medallion" Mold. Plate, 7½"d, Snowbird center decor with Man in the Mountain on three medallions and Snowbird on two, black inner border, heavy gold outer border.

22. Mold 14. "Medallion" Mold. Plate, 8½"d, Reflecting Water Lilies, Shadow Flowers in Medallions.

23. Mold 14. "Medallion" Mold. Oval, open-handled Bowl, 13"x8½", Swallows and Shadow Flowers.

24. Mold 14. "Medallion" Mold. Tray, 11½", Snowbird center decor with Sheepherder, Man in the Mountain, and Snowbird scenes on medallions, black inner border, heavy gold outer border.

25. Mold 14a. "Medallion" Mold Variation. Bowl, 9½"d, Lebrun center with Madame Récamier, Lebrun, and Countess Potocka in oval reserves on border, cobalt blue inner border, gold tapestry work on outer border.

26. Mold 14a. "Medallion" Mold Variation. Bowl, 11"d, Hanging Basket, undecorated oval reserves on border.

27. Mold 16. "Plume" Mold. Bowl, 11"d, Poppies and Morning Bells.

28. Mold 18. "Ribbon and Jewel" Mold. Tray, 12"x7½", Reflecting Poppies and Daisies.

29. Mold 18. "Ribbon and Jewel" Mold. Bowl, 10½"d, Roses with Floral Garlands on border, satin finish.

30. Mold 18. "Ribbon and Jewel" Mold. Bowl, 10½"d, Masted Ship.

31. Mold 18. "Ribbon and Jewel" Mold. Plate, 8½"d, Melon Eaters, gold stencilled designs on inner border, lavender Tiffany finish on outer border.

32. Mold 18. "Ribbon and Jewel" Mold. Tray, 12"l, pearl luster finish.

33. Mold 18. "Ribbon and Jewel" Mold. Plate 8½"d, Dice Throwers.

34. Mold 19. "Sea Creature" Mold. Bowl, 11″d, Roses, unmarked.

35. Mold 22. "Square and Jewel" Mold. Bowl, 11″d, Reflecting Poppies and Daisies.

36. Mold 23. "Stippled Floral" Mold. Bowl, 9¾"d, Lebrun, unmarked.

37. Mold 23. "Stippled Floral" Mold. Pair of Plates, 6"d, Victorian Vignettes: Lady Feeding Chickens and Seated Lady with Fan, unmarked.

38. Mold 23. "Stippled Floral" Mold. Pair of Plates, 6"d Victorian Vignettes: Lady with Dog and Lady Watering Flowers, unmarked.

Popular Named Floral Molds and Other Popular Named Molds (Photographs 39 to 70)

39. Mold 25. "Iris" Mold. Cake Plate, 11"d, cobalt blue background, Poppies.

40. Mold 25. "Iris" Mold. Cake Plate, 11"d, Poppies.

41. Mold 25. "Iris" Mold. Bowl, 9½"d, (Bowl in a Bowl), Roses, gold trim on outer border.

42. Mold 26. "Iris" Mold Variation. Bowl, 9"d, Mixed Florals. This example has RSP Mark 4. Only unmarked pieces in this mold were shown in Book I.

43. Mold 28. "Carnation" Mold. Berry Set: Master Bowl, 9″d; Individual Bowls (6), 5½″d, Roses.

44. Mold 28. "Carnation" Mold. Cake Plate, 11″d, Magnolias.

45. Mold 28. "Carnation" Mold. Bowl, 10½″d, lavender Tiffany finish on Carnations, pink and white Roses.

46. Mold 28a. "Carnation" Mold Variation. Bowl, 10½″d, multicolored flowers, gold stencilled designs inner bowl, heavy gold outer border.

47. Mold 30. "Lily" Mold (Square Version). Footed Bowl, 7"d, portrait decor, bronze iridescent Tiffany finish unmarked.

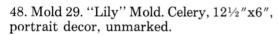

48. Mold 29. "Lily" Mold. Celery, 12½"x6", portrait decor, unmarked.

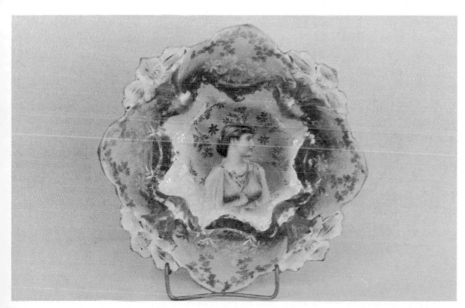

49. Mold 30. "Lily" Mold (Square Version). Footed Bowl, 7"d, portrait decor, unmarked.

50. Mold 29. "Lily" Mold. Cake Plate, 10½"d, Mixed Florals, unmarked.

51. Mold 29. "Lily" Mold. Bowl, 10½"d, Roses, unmarked.

52. Mold 29. "Lily" Mold. Footed Bowl, 10½"d (ten petal feet), Roses and Shadow Flowers, unmarked.

53. Mold 29a. "Lily" Mold Variation. Bowl, 11"d, Primroses, Tiffany finish on border, satin finish interior.

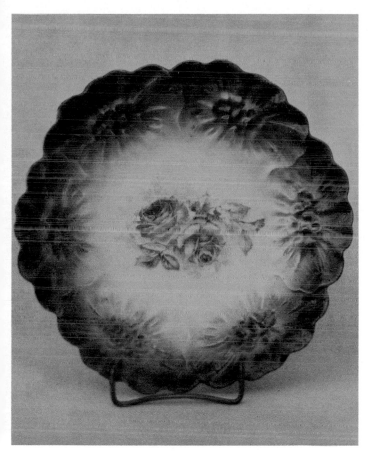

54. Mold 31. "Sunflower" Mold. Plate, 9"d, Roses.

55. Mold 32. "Berry" Mold (clumps of berry-like designs on outer border). Cake Plate, 10"d, Roses.

56. Mold 32a. "Berry" Mold Variation (clusters of Berries alternate with blown-out dome shapes on border). Bowl, 10½"d, Roses.

57. Mold 32b. "Berry" Mold Variation (small clusters of berries with leaves embossed around inside border). Bowl, 11"d, Roses.

58. Mold 33. "Bleeding Heart" Mold. Bowl, 10½"d, pink and white flowers.

59. Mold 34. "Honeycomb" Mold (note "Honeycomb" stippled work around the blown-out dome shapes). Bowl, 10¾"d, Roses.

60. Mold 34. "Honeycomb" Mold. Cake Plate, 10½"d, Hanging Basket.

61. Mold 35. "Locket" Mold (concave oval designs around inside border). Bowl, 10"d, satin finish.

62. Mold 35a. "Locket" Mold Variation ("locket" shapes are convex). Bowl, 10½"d, satin finish.

63. Mold 35b. "Locket" Mold Variation ("locket" shapes around inner border). Bowl, 10"d, pastel florals center decor, Colonial portraits in lockets.

64. Mold 36. "Pie Crust" Mold (ribbed border). Berry Set: Master Bowl, 9¼"d; Individual Bowls (6), Lily of the Valley, satin finish.

65. Mold 37. "Shield" Mold (recessed convex shapes extending into bowl). Bowl, 10½"d, yellow Roses.

66. Mold 37. "Shield" Mold. Bowl, 10½"d, Roses.

67. Mold 37a. "Shield" Mold Variation. Bowl, 11"d, Hanging Basket.

68. Mold 38. "Strawberry" Mold (embossed berries around inside border). Cake Plate, 11½"d, Poppies, pearl luster finish.

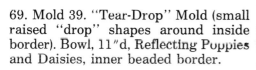

69. Mold 39. "Tear-Drop" Mold (small raised "drop" shapes around inside border). Bowl, 11"d, Reflecting Poppies and Daisies, inner beaded border.

70. Mold 40. "Tulip and Ribbon" Mold (embossed tulip in body). Nut Dish, 4½"d, Roses.

Floral Border Molds (Photographs 71 to 75)

71. Mold 55. Bowl, 10½″d, Autumn figural decor.

72. Mold 56. Plate, 8½″d, Jewels decorated as opals, Roses.

73. Mold 56. Relish, 9½″x5″, undecorated Jewels, Roses.

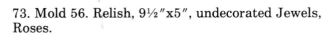

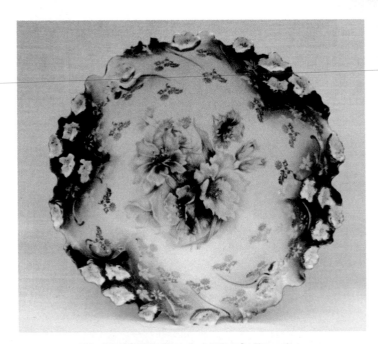

75. Mold 58. Bowl, 10″d, violet floral and leaf garland with apricot and white blossoms, gold trim.

74. Mold 57. Bowl, 10½″d, Poppies.

Unusual Body Shapes (Photographs 76 to 106

76. Mold 78. Tray, 12″l, 7½″w, Magnolias, Wheelock, Mark 51.

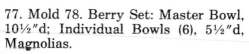

77. Mold 78. Berry Set: Master Bowl, 10½″d; Individual Bowls (6), 5½″d, Magnolias.

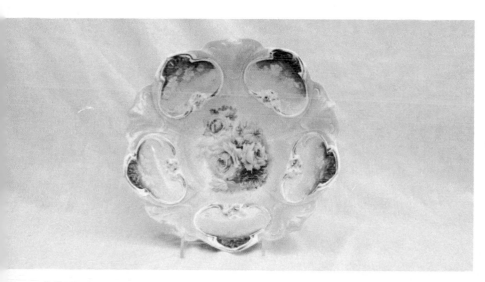

78. Mold 79. Bowl, 10¾″d, Roses.

79. Mold 82. Plate, 9″d, Scattered Flowers decor, Jewels decorated as opals.

80. Mold 82. Bun Tray, 13″x8½″, Scattered Flowers decor, Jewels decorated as opals.

81. Mold 82. Relish, 9½″x4½″, Roses, satin finish, Jewels decorated as opals.

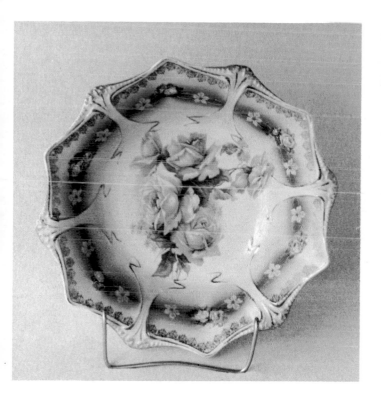

83. Mold 85. Bowl, 10½″d, unusual three scenes: Summer portrait with Cottage and Shadow Buildings in far background.

82. Mold 83. Bowl, 10¾″d, yellow Roses, satin finish.

4. Mold 91. Plate, 8½″d, Mixed Florals, heavy gold trim.

85. Mold 91. Bowl, 10½″d, Mixed Florals with Roses and Snowballs.

86. Mold 93. Plate, 8½"d, Roses.

87. Mold 94. Bowl, 10¾"d, Poppies, watered silk finish, heavy gold trim.

88. Mold 94. Bowl, 11"d, Magnolias, unmarked.

89. Mold 98. Bowl, 10¼″d, Victorian Vignette: Lady Feeding Chickens, unmarked.

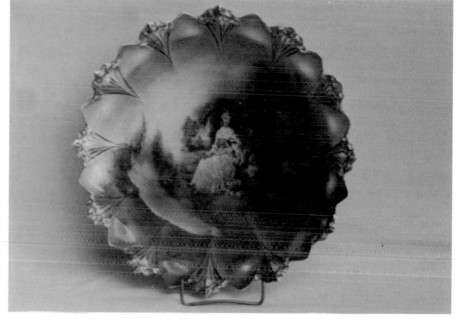

90. Mold 98. Bowl, 10¼″d, Lady with Dog, unmarked.

91. Mold 98. Bowl, 10¼″d, Lady Watering Flowers, unmarked.

92. Mold 98. Bowl, 10½"d, Cottage scene with green and brown background, unmarked.

93. Mold 98. Bowl, 10"d, floral decor in center and on dome shapes, unmarked.

94. Mold 98. Celery, 12½"x5¾", Mixed Florals gold stencilled designs inner border, unmarked.

95. Mold 99 (rounded dome shapes alternate with pointed domes, separated by fanned rib shapes). Berry Set: Master Bowl, 11″d; Individual Bowls (6), 5″d, Roses with Shadow Flowers.

96. Mold 100 (five large domes with embossed flower and stem in each, separated by smaller scalloped sections. Note interior of Mold is pentagon shaped). Bowl, 11″d, Poppies.

97. Mold 101 (five large domes extending toward center of piece; recessed flower and stems within each dome; domes separated by smaller scalloped sections). Bowl, 10½″d, Mixed Florals.

98. Mold 102 (ten domes separated by pointed convex shapes, ribbed at top; eight petal floral design molded into interior of body). Bowl, 10½″d, rare Four Seasons decor, raised gold outlines interior petal mold.

99. Mold 103 (five recessed dome shapes, scalloped outer border). Bowl 10½"d, white flowers.

100. Mold 104 (eight recessed shallow pointed domes alternating with small rounded shapes). Bowl, 10½"d, Roses, pearl luster finish.

101. Mold 105 (five large rounded dome shapes separated by irregular wavy shapes). Bowl, 10½"d, Sheepherder scenic decor.

102. Mold 106 (five recessed domes alternating with fleur-de-lys sections). Bowl, 10"d, Lilacs and Surreal Dogwood Blossoms.

103. Mold 107 (six shallow domes separated by embossed "drops," irregular lightly scalloped border). Cake Plate, 11″d, Tulips, matte finish.

104. Mold 108 (six domes with raised centers, separated by small ribbed fan shapes). Individual Berry Bowl, 5¼″d, pink florals, satin finish.

105. Mold 109 (five double elongated domes alternating with scalloped concave shapes extending toward center). Bowl, 10¼″d, Roses.

106. Mold 110. (six domes separated by fluted, convex shapes). Footed Centerpiece Bowl, 10¼″d, Tulips.

Border Molds (Pointed--Photographs 107 to 110)

107. Mold 154. Berry Set: Master Bowl, 11″d; Individual Bowls (6), Oak Leaves, satin finish.

108. Mold 154. Bowl, 9″d, pink Roses, gold leaves with red trim, satin finish.

109. Mold 155. Bowl, 11″d, Turkeys, Ducks, and Swallows.

110. Mold 155. Tray, 11½″x7½″, Mill scene with Swallows.

Border Molds (Rounded Scallops--Photographs 111 to 115)

111. Mold 181a (Bowl size for this Mold determines number of individual rounded scallops). Bowl, 7¼"d, pierced handle, Swallows and Water Lilies.

112. Mold 182. Plate, 7½"d, Roses, satin finish.

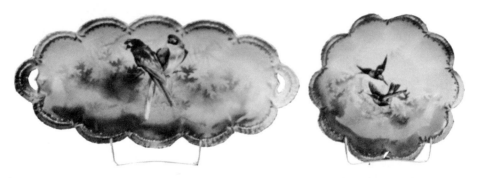

113. Mold 182. Relish, 9½"x4½", Parrots; Berry Bowl, 5¼"d, Hummingbirds.

114. Mold 182. Berry Set: Master Bowl, 10"d; Individual Bowls (6), 5½"d, Fruit decor with fruit sliced open, unmarked. (Peeled or sliced-open fruit is considered to be a rare decoration.)

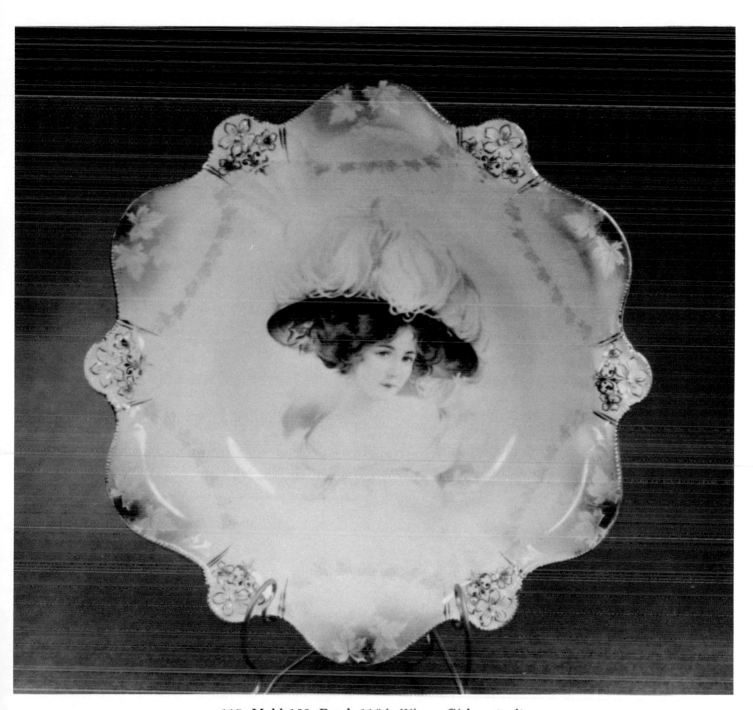

115. Mold 183. Bowl, 11″d, Gibson Girl portrait.

Border Molds (Semi-round Scallops--Photographs 116 to 129)

116. Mold 202. Plate, 8½″d, Sand Snipe.

117. Mold 202. Plate, 9″d, Poppies.

118. Mold 205. Relish, 12½″l, pink and white Canterbury Bells, pearl luster finish.

119. Mold 205. Cake Plate, 10¼″d, Snow Drops.

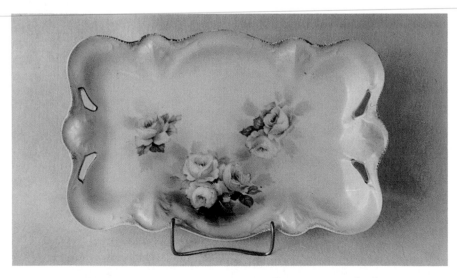

120. Mold 205. Tray, 11½″x7½″, Roses, unmarked.

121. Mold 205. Bowl, 10½″d, scenic Swans and Terrace decor.

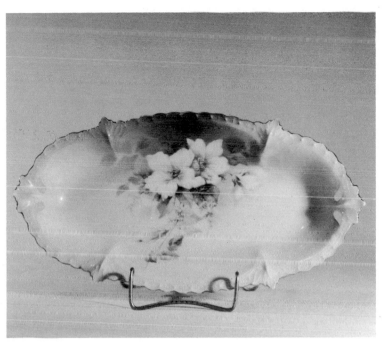

122. Mold 207. Cake Plate, 11½"d, Scattered Flowers, Jewels decorated as opals.

123. Mold 210. Celery, 12"x6½", Lilies.

124. Mold 211. Bowl, 10½"d, Poppies, Wheelock, Mark 51.

125. Mold 211a. Bowl, 10½"d, Winter figural decor.

126. Mold 211a. Bowl, 10½″d, Roses.

127. Mold 212. Bowl, 10″d, orange and white flowers, satin finish.

128. Mold 213. Cake Plate, 10¼″d, Roses and Snowballs.

129. Mold 214 (fleur-de-lys separate the semi-rounded scallops). Bowl, 10¼″d, very faint rose decor in center.

Border Molds (Crimped Scallops--Photographs 130 to 141)

130. Mold 252. Bowl, 11"d, Daisies, watered silk finish, unmarked.

131. Mold 253. Bowl, 10½"d, Farm Scene.

132. Mold 253a (the sections separating the domes are convex rather than concave). Plate, 9"d, Canterbury Bells.

133. Mold 254. Bowl, 10½"d, Roses.

134. Mold 256. Berry Bowl, 5½″d, Stag with Shadow Flowers.

135. Mold 259. Bowl, 9″d, Roses.

137. Mold 261. Plate, 8½″d, Bird of Paradise.

136. Mold 260 (pierced holes on each side of crimped scallop sections). Bowl, 10½″d, Mixed Floral decor.

138. Mold 262 (deeply crimped fan shapes extend toward center and divide the larger sections, domes are recessed below outer border). Bowl, 10½"d, Roses.

139. Mold 263 (lightly crimped outer border, semi-oval recessed sections around inner border). Plate, 8½"d, Snowballs and Roses.

140. Mold 264. Berry Set: Master Bowl, 9"d; Individual Bowls (5), 5"d; Lily of the Valley decor.

141. Mold 265. Cake Plate, 11½"d, Dogwood and Pine.

Border Molds (Wavy Scallops--Photographs 142 to 145)

142. Mold 276. Celery, 12½″x6¼″, Dogwood and Pine.

143. Mold 277. Plate, 7½″d, pink and white flowers, Tiffany iridescent finish around border.

144. Mold 277. Cake Plate, 11½″d, Roses and Daisies.

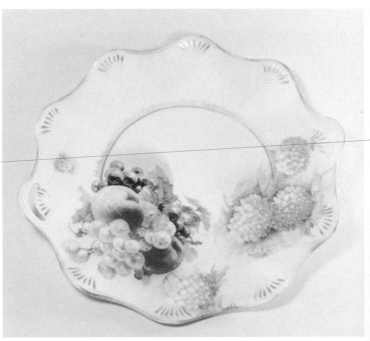

145. Mold 278 (ribbed designs under wavy scallops). Cake Plate, 12″d, unusual decoration of Fruit and Snowballs. There is also a faint image of a coffee pot in the center of the plate.

146. Mold 302a (fan sections separating scallops are larger than in Mold 302). Bowl, 10″d, Snowballs.

147. Mold 303. Bowl, 10½″d, Roses.

148. Mold 304. Cake Plate, 9½″d, Roses, satin finish.

149. Mold 304. Celery, 12″x6″, Man in the Mountain, unmarked.

150. Mold 304. Celery, 12″x6″, two scenes: Sheepherder and Swallows.

151. Mold 304. Bowl, 11″d, Reflecting Water Lilies, cobalt blue background, Wheelock, Mark 51.

152. Mold 304. Cake Plate, 9½″d, Peacock and Ducks.

153. Mold 304. Plate, 8½″d, three scenes: Turkeys, Swans, and Swallows.

154. Mold 304. Celery, 12½″l, three scenes: Barnyard Animals, Swans, and Swallows.

155. Mold 304. Footed Bowl, 6″d, three scenes: Pheasant, Swans, and Swallows.

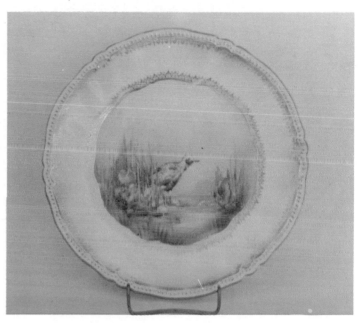

156. Mold 305. Cake Plate, 9½"d, Roses.

157. Mold 306. Plate, 8½"d, Water Bird and Marsh.

158. Mold 306. Plate, 8½"d, Girl with Letter (one of the Four Charmers), satin finish.

159. Mold 306. Bowl, 9"d, floral center with Cherubs on three reserves around inner border.

161. Mold 308 (wavy elongated scallops separated by small ribbed indentations). Tray, 12½"x9", Lily of the Valley.

160. Mold 307 (small pointed shapes separate elongated scallops). Bowl, 11"d, pink and white flowers, satin finish.

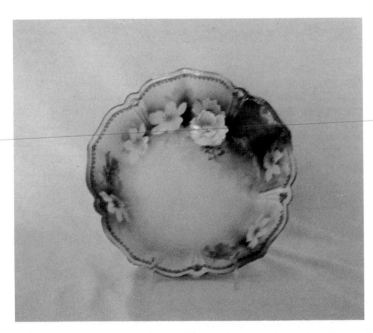

162. Mold 309 (small rounded scallops separate large elongated sections). Bowl, 10"d, white flowers, satin finish.

163. Mold 310 (small indentations with jewels separate elongated scallops). Bowl, 10"d, Roses with Carnations on border and one at base, five Jewels decorated as rubies.

Border Molds (Irregular Scallops--Photographs 164 to 185)

164. Mold 329. Bowl, 10¾″d, Scattered Flowers.

165. Mold 334. Bowl, 11″d, Reflecting Water Lilies.

166. Mold 340. Bowl, 10½″d, Asters, iridescent Tiffany finish on fan shapes around border.

167. Mold 341. Cake Plate, 10″d, white flowers.

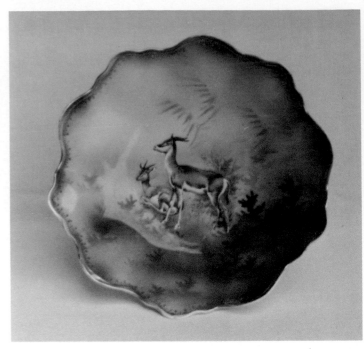

168. Mold 341. Compote, 7½″d, (pedestal base not shown), Gazelles, rare decoration.

169. Mold 341. Footed Bowl, 5¼″d, Violets.

170. Mold 341. Footed Bowl, 7¼″d, Grape and Leaf decor.

171. Mold 341. Plate, 8¾″d, Lily with Maidenhair Fern, pearl luster finish, unmarked.

172. Mold 341. Cake Plate, 10″d, Violets, satin finish.

174. Mold 343. Celery, 12"x6", Seated Lady with Fan and scenic decor, Surreal Dogwood Blossoms inner border, unmarked.

173. Mold 342. Cake Plate, 11½"d, multicolored Poppies.

175. Mold 343. Cake Plate, 10½"d, Diana the Huntress center with Cupids in reserves on border, iridescent Tiffany finish on border.

176. Mold 343. Bun Tray, Cobalt Blue border, Roses, gold trim, Mark 52 (Viersa Crown Mark).

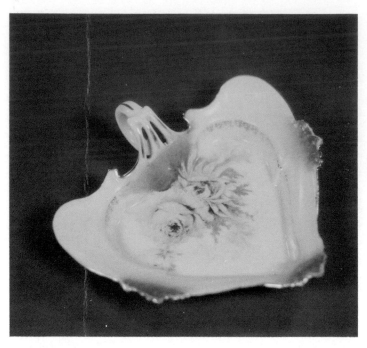

177. Mold 344 (Heart shape). Receiving Card Tray, 6″x6″, Rose and Daisy.

178. Mold 345. Bowl, 10½″d, Iris.

179. Mold 346. Bowl, 10½″d, Hanging Basket.

180. Mold 346. Celery, 12½″x6″, pink and white flowers, lavender iridescent finish on part of lower border.

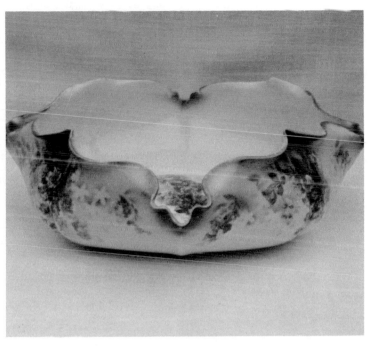

181. Mold 347. Bowl, 9½"d, Poppies with gold Burrs and Leaves.

182. Mold 348. Bowl, 10"d, pink flowers decorate center and exterior, gold trim.

183. Mold 349. Celery, 11½"l, Admiral Peary Arctic scene, "Midst Snow and Ice" printed in lower right hand corner.

184. Mold 350. Bowl, 10"d, white Roses and Shadow Flowers, satin finish.

185. Mold 351. Bowl, 11″d, white and peach flowers, satin finish center, iridescent Tiffany bronze finish on border.

Border Molds (Scroll Borders--Photographs 186 and 187)

186. Mold 404. Bowl, 8½"d, Magnolias.

187. Mold 405. Bowl, 10½"d, Sitting Basket.

Border Molds (Smooth Borders--Photographs 188 and 189)

188. Mold 426a. Plate, 10"d, scenic design on Country House and Lake with figures on the bank.

189. Mold 428. Tray, 11"x7", Cotton Bolls.

190. Mold 452a (Mold is similar to Mold 452 except body ribbing is straight and there is a beaded border at base). Chocolate Pot, 10″h, large Magnolia Blossom.

192. Mold 457. Chocolate Pot, 10″h, Sugar, 4½″h, Creamer, 3½″h, Roses and Snowballs.

191. Mold 456. Pitcher, 9½″h, Poppies.

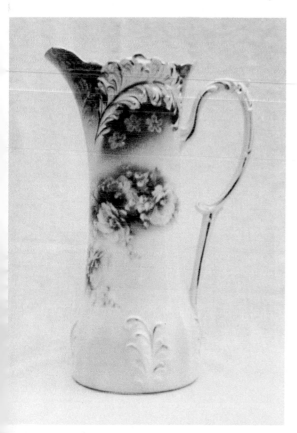

193. Mold 465 (Plume Mold). Pitcher, 8½″h, Poppies.

194. Mold 466 (Icicle Mold). Tankard, 11¾″h, Reflecting Water Lilies.

195. Mold 466 (Icicle Mold). Cup and Saucer, Reflecting Poppies and Daisies.

196. Mold 467 (also see Mold 304 in Flat Objects, Photographs 148-155; Mold 584, Photograph 299 in Vertical Objects; and Mold 804, Photograph 383 in Accessories). Demi-tasse Cup, 2½"h, and Saucer, Roses.

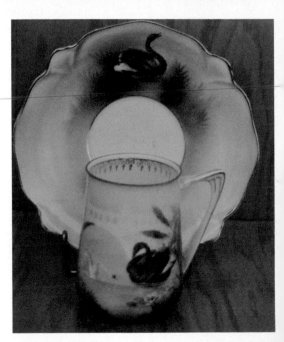

197. Mold 468. Demi-tasse Cup, 2½"h, and Saucer, white and green floral and leaf garlands.

198. Mold 469. (also see Mold 253a, Photograph 132 in Flat Objects). Demi-tasse Cup and Saucer, Black and White Swans.

199. Mold 470. Egg Warmer, 2½"h, small pink flowers on borders.

200. Mold 471. Tea Strainer, pink and white flowers.

201. Mold 472. Demi-tasse Cup, 3"h, pink Roses and Surreal Dogwood Blossoms.

202. Mold 473 (Lily of the Valley Mold). Tea Pot, 7½"h, pink Roses and white lilies. Lilies of the Valley molded into body at top, extending into handle.

203. Mold 474. Demi-tasse Set: Coffee Pot, 9″h, Cups, 2″h, Roses.

204. Mold 474. Demi-tasse Coffee Pot, 9″h, Dogwood and Pine.

205. Mold 474. Demi-tasse Coffee Pot, 9″h, Roses.

206. Mold 475. Jam Jar, 4¼″h, Calla Lily, RSP Mark with BT Co, Mark 45.

207. Mold 476. Syrup Pitcher 5½″h and Underplate, Swans and Terrace.

208. Mold 477. Cracker Jar, 7½″h, Farm Scene on each side.

209. Mold 478. Jam Jar, 3¾″h, white Roses.

210. Mold 501. Cup, 2½″h, Roses.

211. Mold 501. Lemonade Pitcher, 6″h, large pink Shadow Flowers, unmarked.

212. Mold 501. Chocolate Set: Chocolate Pot, 10″h, Cups, 3¼″h, multicolored Roses.

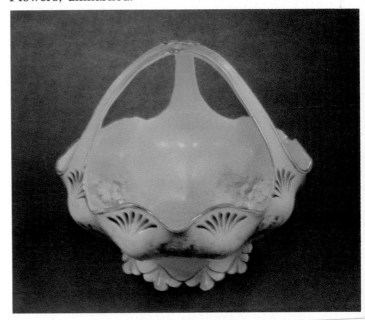

213. Mold 501. Basket, three handled, white floral decor.

214. Mold 501. Centerpiece Bowl, white flowers interior and exterior.

215. Mold 501. Spooner, 3½″h, green leaf chains and Roses. RSP Mark with "Dresden," Mark 46.

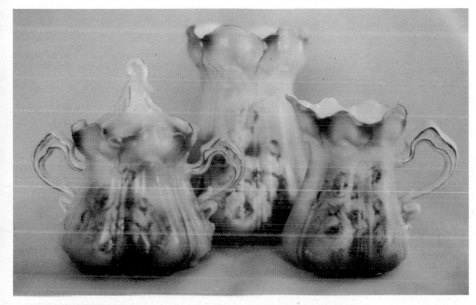

216. Mold 502. Spooner, Sugar and Creamer, Poppies.

217. Mold 503. Cracker Jar, 7"h, multicolored flowers.

218. Mold 503. Syrup Pitcher, 5"h, multicolored flowers, satin finish.

219. Mold 505. Sugar, 4"h, Creamer, 2½"h, Roses. (This Mold has been reproduced in tea sets. Tea Pots are 7¼"h. The decoration is "Green mist", pink roses on light green background, or "Orchid", large orchid colored flower on light cream background.)

220. Mold 507. Syrup Pitcher, 4¾″h, multicolored flowers.

221. Mold 507. Syrup Pitcher, 4¾″h, Poppies.

222. Mold 507. Centerpiece Bowl, 11″d, Poppies, unmarked.

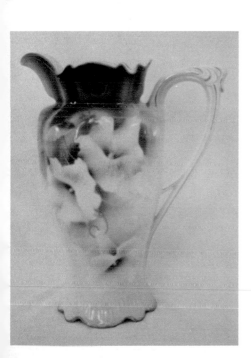

223. Mold 508. Tankard, 11½"h,
Lilies, unmarked.

224. Mold 508. Tankard, white flowers, unmarked.

225. Mold 509a. Syrup, 5″h, Roses.

226. Mold 509a. Syrup, 5″h, Poppies, gold enamelling.

227. Mold 509a. Mustard Pot, 3″h, Poppies.

228. Mold 509b. Cracker Jar, 5½″h, 6″d, Roses.

229. Mold 510. Chocolate Set: Chocolate Pot, 10½"h, Cups (Mold 523), 3½"h, Rose garlands.

230. Mold 510. Chocolate Set: Pot, 10½"h, Cups (Mold 523), 3½"h, Roses and Surreal Dogwood.

231. Mold 510. Cracker Jar, 5½"h, Laurel Chain decor.

232. Mold 512. Sugar and Creamer, 4½"h, multicolored flowers.

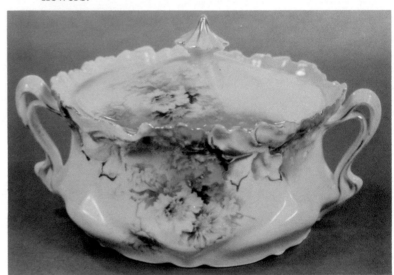

233. Mold 512. Jam Jar, 5"h, Roses, satin finish.

234. Mold 514. Cracker Jar, 6"h, Mixed Florals, unmarked.

235. Mold 515 (Hidden Image Mold). Cup or Shaving Mug, 3½"h, unmarked.

236. Mold 515 (Hidden Image Mold). Pitcher, 5"h, unmarked.

237. Mold 517. Chocolate Pot, 10"h,
Lady with Fan, unmarked.

238. Mold 517. Sugar and Creamer, 5"h,
Lebrun portrait.

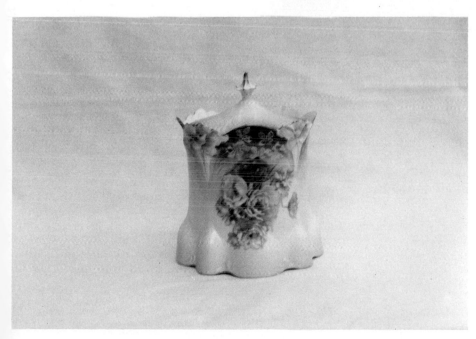

239. Mold 517. Cracker Jar, 7½"h,
Poppies.

240. Mold 517. Tankard, 15″h, Countess Potocka, unmarked.

241. Mold 520. Chocolate Pot, 11¾″h, Madame Récamier, Tiffany bronze finish, unmarked. (A similar mold is being made in a new chocolate pot, 10″h and a covered urn, 12″h with "Wildflower" decor, sprays of pink flowers with green leaves. A coffee pot is also being made with similar decor called "gold medallion.")

242. Mold 521. Spooner, 3½"h, Swans, matte finish.

243. Mold 521. Mustard Pot, 3"h and Ladle, handpainted roses (note this was a blank, not factory decorated), unmarked.

244. Mold 521. Sugar, 5½"h, Creamer, 4"h, Mixed Florals, beaded medallions on front, pearl luster finish.

245. Mold 521. Tea Pot, 6"h, Roses.

246. Mold 522 (Ribbon and Jewel Mold). Pitcher, 9½"h, Roses and Snowballs, Jewel decorated as an opal.

247. Mold 525 (Stippled Floral Mold). Tankard, 13"h, Summer portrait with Cottage scene in background.

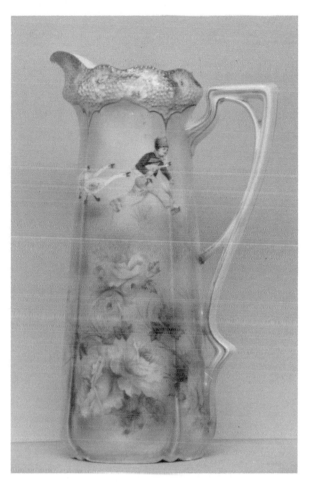

248. Mold 525 (Stippled Floral Mold). Tankard, 14"h, Boy with Geese, Roses, watered silk finish, unmarked.

249. Mold 525 (Stippled Floral Mold). Tankard, 13"h, Fruit decor. Wheelock, Mark 51.

250. Mold 525 (Stippled Floral Mold), Tankard, 13"h, Poppies, unmarked.

251. Mold 525 (Stippled Floral Mold). Tea Set: Tea Pot, 7″h, Sugar, 4¾″h, Creamer, 3¾″h, Clematis, unmarked.

252. Mold 525 (Stippled Floral Mold). Cracker Jar, 3½″x9″, Fruit decor, unmarked.

253. Mold 525 (Stippled Floral Mold). Sugar, 5″h, Mixed Florals.

254. Mold 525 (Stippled Floral Mold). Creamer, Lilies, unmarked.

255. Mold 526 (Carnation Mold). Chocolate
Pot, 11¾″h, Roses.

256. Mold 526 (Carnation Mold). Toothpick Holder,
Roses.

257. Mold 526 (Carnation Mold). Lemonade Pitcher,
9½″h, Roses.

258. Mold 527. Demi-tasse Sugar and Creamer, Mixed Flowers.

259. Mold 529. Mustard Pot, 4″h, Dogwood Blossoms.

261. Mold 529. Mustard Pot, 4″h, Dogwood and Pine.

260. Mold 529. Chocolate Set: Chocolate Pot, 11″h, Cups (6), 3½″h, Dogwood and Pine. (Also see Mold 276, Photograph 142 in Flat Objects and Mold 881, Photograph 402.)

262. Mold 529. Salt Shaker, 2″h, Dogwood and Pine, unmarked.

263. Mold 529a. Cracker Jar, 7″x5½″, Poppies.

264. Mold 530. Cup, 2½″h, White Flowers.

265. Mold 531 (square scalloped base). Cup, 2½″h, Roses.

266. Mold 532. Cracker Jar, 8½″h, Mixed Flowers.

267. Mold 533. Lemonade Pitcher, 5½″x8¾″, Roses.

268. Mold 534. Creamer, 3½″h, Lily.

269. Mold 535. Sugar, 4″h, Mill scene.

270. Mold 536 (also see Mold 259, Photograph 135 in Flat Objects; and Mold 861, Photograph 395 in Accessories). Cracker Jar, 5″x9½″, Roses, iridescent lavender Tiffany finish.

271. Mold 537. Lemonade Pitcher, 6½″h, pink and white Roses.

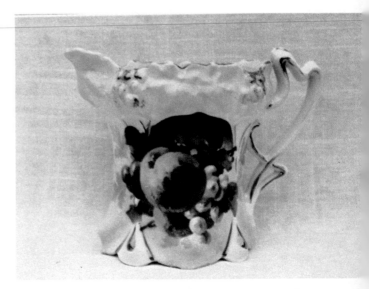

272. Mold 538. Creamer, 3½″h, Fruit decor.

273. Mold 539. Demi-tasse Pot, 9½"h, Rose Garland Wreaths, glossy finish.

274. Mold 540. Demi-tasse Pot, 9½"h, Roses, gold enamelled stems and burrs, satin finish.

275. Mold 540a (handle shape is different from Mold 540). Sugar, 5½"h, Creamer, 4½"h, Swans and Gazebo.

276. Mold 540a. Cracker Jar, Sliced Fruit decor, unmarked.

277. Mold 540a. Syrup, 6½"h, Dogwood Blossoms.

278. Mold 540a. Salt and Pepper Shakers and Toothpick Holder, Roses.

279. Mold 541. Cracker Jar, 7″h, Mill scene.

280. Mold 542. Pitcher, 6″h, Poppies.

281. Mold 543. Salt and Pepper Shakers, 2½″h, white Lily decor.

282. Mold 543. Salt Shaker, 2½″h, Mixed Flowers.

283. Mold 544. Demi-tasse Cup and Saucer, cameo portrait f Colonial Man, small pink flowers, gold trim.

284. Mold 545. Syrup, 4″h, Roses.

285. Mold 546. Chocolate Set: Chocolate Pot, 11″h, Cups, 3½″h, Lily decor with blue-green Tiffany finish at top.

286. Mold 547. Demi-tasse Set: Pot, 8″h, Cups (5), 2″h, Snowballs.

287. Mold 548. Chocolate Set: Pot, 10″h, Mixed Flowers, satin finish.

288. Mold 549. Chocolate Set: Pot, 12″h, Cups (5), 3½″h, Clematis.

289. Mold 550. Child's Set: Cake Plates (2), 5½″d, Sugar, 3″h, Tea Pot, 5″h, Creamer, 2″h, Cobalt Blue border, yellow Roses, unmarked.

290. Chocolate Pot, Coffee Cup, and Chocolate Cup, Mold 509a; Cake Plate, Mold 251. Roses, Tiffany bronze inner border, satin finish.

291. Mold 577. Tea Set: Pot, 7½"h, Creamer, 5"h, Sugar, 5½"h, Cherubs, satin finish.

292. Mold 577. Creamer, 4½"h, Roses.

293. Mold 579. Syrup, 6"h, Roses, glossy finish.

294. Mold 579. Lemonade Pitcher, 6½"x9", Canterbury Bells.

295. Mold 580. Sugar and Creamer, 4½"h, Castle scene.

296. Mold 581. Sugar, 5½"x6", white and pink floral sprays.

297. Mold 582. Tankard, 13″h, three scenes: Ducks, Swans, and Swallows.

298. Mold 583 (Acorn and Leaf shapes embossed on base). Tankard, 11″h, Poppies.

299. Mold 584 (also see Mold 304, Photographs 148-155 in Flat Objects; Mold 467, Photograph 196 in Vertical Objects; and Mold 804, Photograph 383 in Accessories). Tankard, 13½″h, Hanging Basket.

300. Mold 584. Tankard, Swans and Evergreens.

301. Mold 585 (iris in relief forms handle). Tankard, 11½"h, Cottage scene, unmarked.

302. Mold 585. Tankard, 11½″h, Lebrun portrait, pearl luster finish, unmarked.

303. Mold 586 (fancy scalloped base). Tankard, 11½″h, Roses and Snowballs. (This mold has been reproduced in a pitcher, 11½″h; the decoration is "Antique Rose," large red and yellow roses.)

304. Mold 601. Tea Set: Tea Pot, 6¼″h, Sugar, 5½″h, Creamer, 4½″h, center floral border, unmarked.

305. Mold 602. Sugar and Creamer, 4″h, Swallows.

306. Mold 603. Sugar and Creamer, 5½″h, lavender and white flowers.

307. Mold 607. Sugar and Creamer, 4″h, small pink floral sprays.

308. Mold 609 (Fleur-de-lys Mold). Mustard Pot and Ladle, 4"h, Poppies.

309. Mold 610. Cream Soup Cup and Saucer, Dogwood Blossoms.

310. Mold 610. Cup, Roses, gold trim.

311. Mold 611. Creamer, 4"h, white Narcissus.

111

312. Mold 612. Tea Set: Tea Pot, 5¾"h, Sugar, 4¾"h, Creamer, 4"h, green and gold trim, pink roses, satin finish.

313. Mold 613. Centerpiece Bowl, 4½"h, 8"d, lavender floral sprays.

314. Mold 614. Creamer, 4"h, Sugar, 6"h, Roses and Shadow Flowers, unmarked.

315. Mold 615. Sugar and Creamer, 4"h, multicolored floral sprays, unmarked.

316. Mold 616. Tea Sct, Roses. Cups are Mold 510.

317. Mold 617. Coffee Set: Coffee Pot, 7″h, Cups, 2″h, white floral decor.

113

318. Mold 626 (Sunflower Mold). Creamer, 3½″h.

319. Mold 627a. Cup, 2¾″h, Mixed Floral.

320. Mold 627b. Cracker Jar, 6½″h, portrait decor, marble finish, unmarked.

321. Mold 628 (Iris Mold). Toothpick Holder, Poppies.

322. Mold 628 (Iris Mold). Cracker Jar, 7″h, watered silk finish.

323. Mold 628 (Iris Mold). Chocolate Pot, 10½″, Poppies.

324. Mold 631 (Medallion Mold). Tea Set: Tea Pot, 6″h, Covered Creamer, 5″h, Sugar, 5½″h, Diana the Huntress and Flora figural cameos, gold tapestry background, Sitting Basket.

325. Mold 631 (Medallion Mold). Toothpick, Duck and Evergreen, medallion undecorated.

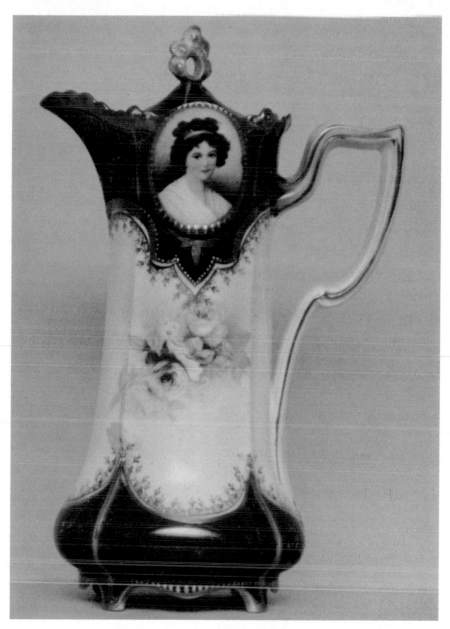

326. Mold 631 (Medallion Mold). Chocolate Pot, 9″h, Lebrun portrait (Countess Potocka on reverse), Cobalt Blue background.

327. Mold 632 (see Mold 862, Photograph 396 in Acessories). Mustache Cup, 3½″h, Poppies.

328. Mold 632. Cracker Jar, 5½″x9″, Pink Flowers with Gold Leaves.

329. Mold 632. Tea Set: Pink Flowers with Gold Leaves.

330. Mold 632. Chocolate Pot, 9″h, Pink Flowers with Gold Leaves.

331. Mold 632. Demi-Tasse Pot, 9″h, multicolored Roses.

332. Mold 635. Cracker Jar, 8½"h, Dogwood and Pine. See Mold 807, Photograph 386 in Accessories. (This Mold has been reproduced in a Cracker Jar, 7½"h, decorated with a portrait of a woman with long brown hair, deep chocolate brown background. The "Sweetheart" transfer is not an RSP subject.)

333. Mold 638. Sugar and Creamer, 4¾"h, colored leaves.

334. Mold 640 (This Mold is still being reproduced in a Ewer, 5½"h. The reproduction is not an exact Mold copy. The decoration is either "English Rose," pink flowers, or "Antique Rose," large yellow and red roses.) Tankard, 12"h, Diana The Huntress, irridescent Tiffany finish, Mark 15.

335. Mold 642. Mustard Pot, 3½"h, with ladle, Roses.

336. Mold 642. Cracker Jar, 7"h, Roses.

337. Mold 643. (A Mold very similar to this is being reproduced in a Chocolate Pot with "Daisy" decoration on a light matte green to cream finish. The finial is pierced and not a floral shape. There are no Jewels.) Toothpick Holder, 2½"h, Flowers in Glass Bowl.

338. Mold 643. Tankard, 15″h, Roses, iridescent Tiffany finish on base.

339. Mold 643. Coffee Pot, 9½″h, Roses, satin finish, Jewels undecorated.

340. Mold 643. Chocolate Set: Chocolate Pot, 10½″h, Creamer, Sugar, Cups and Saucers (10); Milk Pitcher, 5¾″h, Flowers in Glass Bowl.

341. Mold 643. Syrup, 6″h, Roses.

342. Mold 644. Toothpick Holder, Poppies.

343. Mold 644. Cracker Jar, 8″h, Roses.

344. Mold 644. Syrup, 5″h, Roses.

345. Mold 644. Cup or Shaving Mug, 3½″h, Castle scene.

347. Mold 645. Sugar, 5½″h, Creamer, 4″h, Boy with Dog (from the Dice Throwers transfer) and one figure from the Melon Eaters.

346. Mold 645. Demi-tasse Cup, 2½″h and Saucer, mixed flowers, Jewels decorated as opals.

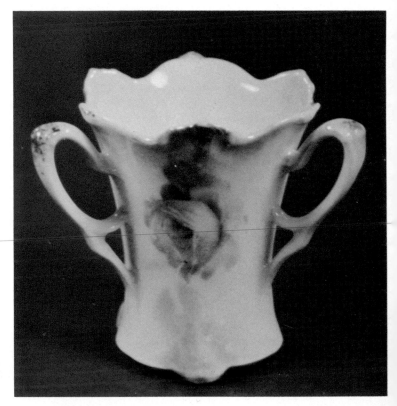

349. Mold 646. Toothpick Holder, 2½″h, Rose decor, unmarked.

348. Mold 646 (ring finial, Jewel at top of Mold, four feet). Chocolate Pot, 9½″h, Snow Drops, pearl luster finish, undecorated Jewel.

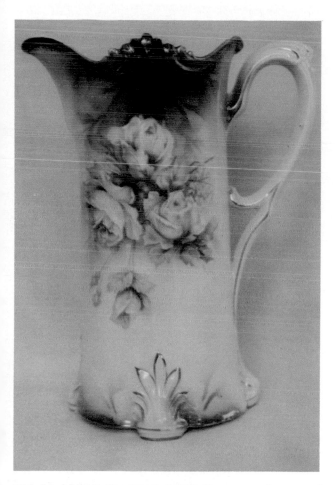

351. Mold 646. Basket, 4″x5½″x4½″, Roses.

350. Mold 646. Tankard, 12″h, Roses, undecorated
Jewel.

352. Mold 647. Sugar and Creamer, 4½″h, Roses.

353. Mold 648. Creamer, 4″h, Lily.

354. Mold 649 (Piecrust Mold). Cracker Jar, 6½″x6½″, Lily of the Valley, satin finish.

355. Mold 649 (Piecrust Mold). Chocolate Set: Chocolate Pot, 10½″h, Cups (2), Lily of the Valley.

356. Mold 650. Sugar and Creamer, 5½″h, floral decor.

357. Mold 651. Sugar and Creamer, 4¾″h, Roses, satin finish.

358. Mold 652. Sugar, 6″h, Creamer, 5½″h, Roses.

359. Mold 653. Cup, 2¼″h and Saucer, Cupid decor in beaded reserve on interior of cup, Roses.

360. Mold 654 (six feet, embossed floral chain around top border). Pitcher, 10"h, Mixed Flowers.

362. Mold 656 (four feet, angular handle). Lemonade Pitcher, 6½″h, Admiral Peary Arctic scene.

361. Mold 655. Lemonade Pitcher, Roses, Wheelock, Mark 51.

363. Mold 657 (Raspberry Mold, berry finial and embossed berries on body). Chocolate Pot, 10″h, Roses, gold accents.

364. Mold 658 (Plume Mold). Demi-tasse Pot, 9″h, Poppies.

Vertical Objects (Applied Feet--Photographs 365 to 367)

365. Mold 702. Sugar, 4½″h, Creamer, 3¼″h, Snowballs and Roses.

366. Mold 704. Mustache Tea Cup, 2½″h, Poppies, pearl luster finish.

367. Mold 704. Footed Bowl, pierced handles, Roses.

368. Mold 726. Hatpin Holder, 4½"h, Mill scene.

369. Mold 728. Hatpin Holder, 4½"h, Swallows.

370. Mold 728. Hatpin Holder, 4½"h, Swans, unmarked.

371. Mold 728. Hatpin Holder, Barnyard Animals.

372. Mold 729. Hatpin Holder, 4½"h, white and green floral decor.

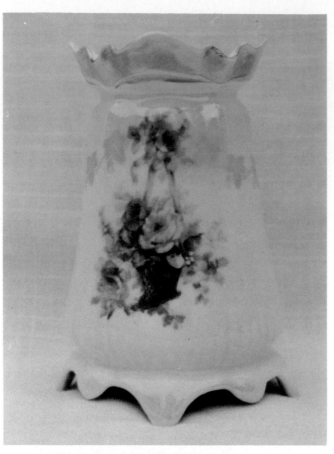

374. Mold 730. Hatpin Holder, 4″h, Roses.

373. Mold 729. Hatpin Holder, 6″h, Hanging Basket II, pearl luster finish.

375. Mold 731. Hatpin Holder, 4¾″h, pink and white flowers.

376. Mold 732. (Also see Mold 656, Photograph 326 in Vertical Objects.) Hatpin Holder, 3¾″h, Admiral Peary Arctic scene.

377. Mold 733. Hatpin Holder, 4¾″h, attached to Pin Box, hairpin molded into top of box, Hanging Basket.

378. Mold 734. Hatpin Holder with attached Pin Box, Roses.

380. Mold 780. Muffineer, 4¾"h, Dogwood and Pine, unmarked.

379. Mold 779. Muffineer, 5½"h, Mixed Flowers, satin finish, unmarked.

381. Mold 781. Muffineer, 5"h, Roses.

382. Mold 782. Muffineer, Roses.

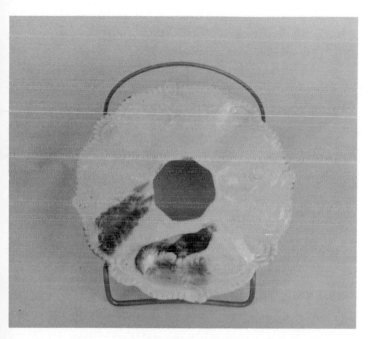

383. Mold 804 (also see Mold 304, Photographs 148-155 in Flat Objects; and Mold 462, Photograph 196 in Vertical Objects). Hair Receiver, 4½"d; Pheasant and Evergreens, pearl luster finish.

384. Mold 805 (also see Mold 507 in Vertical Objects). Hair Receiver, 4½"d, Mixed Flowers.

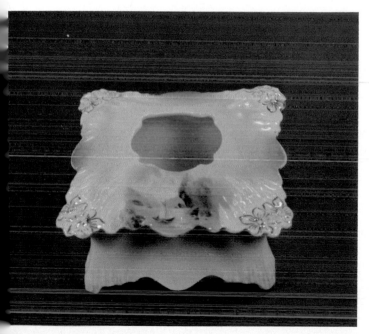

385. Mold 806 (Icicle Mold). Hair Receiver, 4" sq, Man in the Mountain, unmarked.

386. Mold 807 (also see Mold 635, Photograph 332 in Vertical Objects). Hair Receiver, 4"d, Dogwood and Pine.

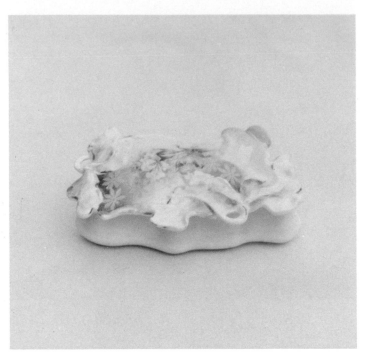

387. Mold 827 (Hidden Image Mold). Pin Box, 4¾″l, Orchids, unmarked.

388. Mold 828. Pin Box, 4″l, Mixed Flowers.

389. Mold 829. Pin Box, 4½″d, Rose decor.

390. Mold 830. Pin Box, 3″sq, Bird of Paradise.

391. Mold 831 (also see Mold 304, Photographs 148-155 in Flat Objects; Mold 462, Photograph 196 in Vertical Objects; and Mold 804, Photograph 383 in Accessories). Pin Box, 5¼"d, Reflecting Water Lilies.

392. Mold 832 (Pin Box), Mold 808 (Hair Receiver); Mold 205 (Tray). Dresser Set, Canterbury Bells.

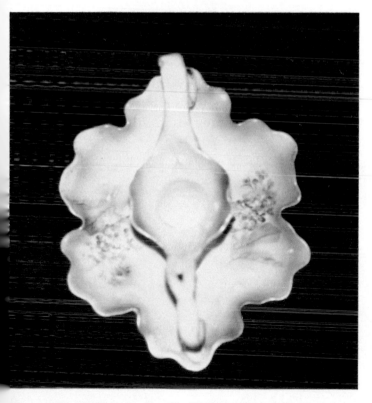

394. Mold 856. Letter Holder, 4¾"h, 4½"w, Mill scene with Swallows, unmarked.

393. Mold 852. Candle Holder, floral decor.

396. Mold 862 (also see Mold 632, Photographs 327-331 in Vertical Objects). Shaving Mug, 3½″h, Pink Flowers with Gold Leaves.

395. Mold 861 (also see Mold 259, Photograph 135 in Flat Objects; and Mold 536, Photograph 270 in Vertical Objects). Shaving Mug, 3½″h, Roses.

397. Mold 863. Shaving Mug with Mirror, 3½″h, Poppies.

398. Mold 864. Shaving Mug, 3½″h, Hanging Basket.

399. Mold 865 (Ribbon and Jewel). Shaving Mug, 3½″h, Roses.

400. Mold 879. Ferner, 6½″h, Lily of the Valley, pearl luster finish.

401. Mold 880. Ferner, 4¼″h, Dogwood and Pine.

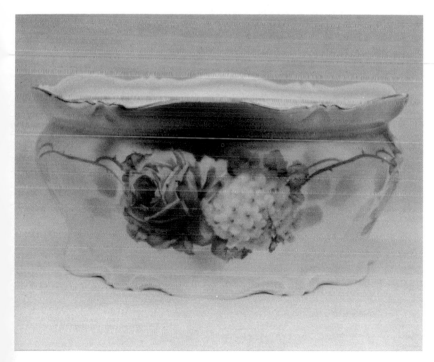

402. Mold 881. Ferner, 5″h, Roses and Snowballs.

403. Mold 882. Ferner with Liner, 3½″h, Poppies.

404. Mold 907. Vase, 6″h, Countess Potocka, Mark 15.

405. Mold 907. Vase, 6″h, Dice Throwers, unmarked.

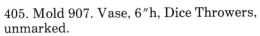

406. Mold 907. Vase, 6″h, Turkeys, unmarked.

407. Mold 909. Vase, 4″h, salesman's sample, Black Swans, unmarked.

408. Mold 909. Vase, 6″h, Peacock.

409. Mold 910. Vase, 8¼″h, Turkeys.

410. Mold 911. Vase, 8¾″h, figural scene: couple with Woman Knitting.

411. Mold 912. Vase, 7¼″h, figural scene: couple with Woman in Swing.

412. Mold 913. Vase, 6″h, figural scene: Peace Bringing Plenty.

414. Mold 914. Vase, 6″h, cameo portrait of Colonial Man.

413. Mold 914. Vase, 4½″h, figural scene: Lady with Dog.

415. Mold 915. Vase, 9″h, Roses and Snowballs.

416. Mold 916 (Grape Mold). Vase, 10¼″h, Winter portrait.

417. Mold 917. Vase, 7¼″h, figural scene: Woman in Swing II.

418. Mold 917. Vase, 7¼″h, figural scene: couple with Woman Knitting.

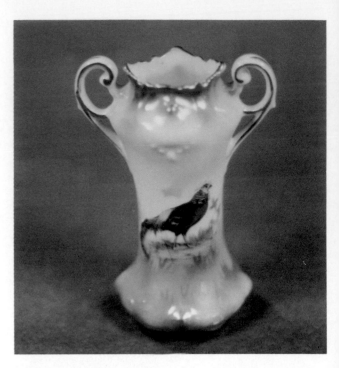

419. Mold 918. Vase, 9″h, figural scene: Woman in Swing II.

420. Mold 918. Vase, 4″h, salesman's sample, Pheasant.

421. Mold 918. Vase, 8″h, figural scene: couple with Woman Knitting.

422. Mold 919. Vase, 8″h, Roses.

423. Mold 920 (Jewels at top and on body). Vase 9″h, Roses, satin finish, Jewels decorated as opals.

424. Mold 921 (Jewels at top and base). Vase, 8½″h, Roses and Snowballs, Jewels decorated as opals.

425. Mold 922. Vase, 9½″h, Roses, white stippled finish.

426. Mold 923 (Art Nouveau shape). Vase, 7″h, Castle scene, Mark 15 with "Germany."

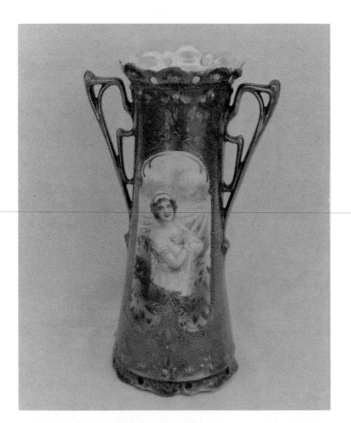

427. Mold 924. Vase, 10¼″h, Spring portrait, iridescent finish.

428. Mold 925. Vase, 9″h, Winter portrait, iridescent Tiffany finish.

429. Mold 926 (floral shapes in high relief). Vase, 9¼″h, Lebrun portrait, Cobalt Blue background, heavy gold accents, unmarked.

430. Mold 927 (similar to Mold 926 but neck and base are different). Vase, 9¼″h, Countess Potocka portrait, Cobalt Blue background, Mark 15.

431. Mold 928. Vase, 6″h, figural scene: The Cage (a reverse position from RSP version I of Boucher's painting).

432. Mold 929 (Fleur-de-lys Mold). Vase, 9″ Winter portrait, lavender iridescent Tiffany finish.

433. Mold 930 (pierced pedestal base with Art Nouveau shaped handles). Vase, 11″h, Roses, iridescent Tiffany finish.

434. Mold 931. Vase, 11″h, Flora figural decor with Cherubs (not shown) on reverse, Mark 15.

435. Mold 932 (Jewels on neck and body). Vase, 9″h, Cottage scene.

436. Mold 933. Loving Cup, 5″h, figural scene: Lady with Fan, unmarked.

437. Mold 934 (Jewels at top and base). Covered Urn, 9¾″h, Roses and Snowballs, watered silk finish, Jewels decorated as opals.

8. Erdmann Schlegelmilch's ES Marked Porcelain
(Photographs 438 to 524)

438. Tankard, 15″h, rococo shape, gold floral decor, red outlining, Mark 37, E. S. Suhla Bird mark in brown.

439. Cracker Jar, intricate pierced overlay work o[...] sides, floral decor on tapestry body finish, Mark 3[...] E. S. Bird mark in brown.

440. Ewer, 7¾"h, "Dragon" shaped handle, Mark 36, E. S. Bird mark in brown.

442. Cognac Bottle, ornate design in Moorish style, Mark 36, E. S. Bird mark in brown.

441. Milk Pitcher, 4½"h, pink stylized flower on turquoise background, Mark 35, ES script mark in brown.

443. Plate, 8"d, fancy scalloped border, stylized white flowers on green background, beaded frame design in center, Mark 23, ES Germany Crown mark in green.

444. Plate 10"d, Girl with Wheat and Sickle, gold stencilled designs, Mark 23.

445. Chocolate Set: Chocolate Pot, 9¼"h, 5 Cups and Saucers, multicolored Mums, Mark 22, ES Germany Royal Saxe mark in green.

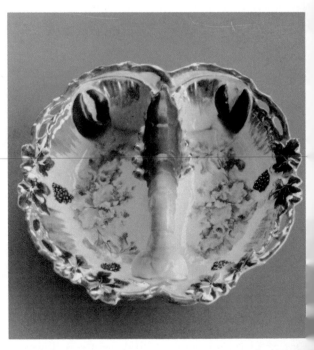

446. Lobster Dish, 9"w, pierced on four sides, pearl luster finish, Mark 22.

447. Vase, 11½"h, Classical figural decor, wine background, Mark 22.

448. Ewer, 12"h, portrait of Woman with Daisy Crown, turquoise borders and beading, pearl luster finish, Mark 22.

449. Vase, 7½"h, portrait decor, finish and frame match Ewer in #448, Mark 23, ES Germany Crown mark.

450. Toothpick Holder, 2½"h, Woman with Daisy Crown, Mark 23.

451. Chamberstick, 2"h, 6"d, Indian Theme: Left Hand Bear, Mark 22, ES Royal Saxe mark.

452. Chamberstick, 2"h, 6"d, blue flowers, Cobalt Blue inner border, Mark 22.

453. Toothpick Holder, 2½"h, Indian Theme: Chief Spotted Horse, Mark 22.

454. Plate, 7½"d, Indian theme: Left Hand Bear with Indian symbols in gold on orange background, Mark 22.

455. Plate, 7¼"d, Indian theme: Sitting Bull, Mark 22.

456. Vase, 6"h, Indian theme: Chief Spotted Horse, Mark 23.

457. Vase, 12″h, very elaborate mold with Gargoyles in relief at base of handles, Lady with Doves figural subject, pearl luster finish, Mark 38 (mark has similar numbers as the ES Germany Crown mark) with Royal Windsor.

458. Bowl, 11½"d, open handles, figural decor, Goddess of the Sea, green pearl luster finish, Prov Sxe Mark 20.

459. Bowl, 11¾"d, open handles, pierced border, Woman Holding Flowers, Prov Sxe Mark 20.

460. Small Dish, 5¼"d, open work around inner border with molded leaves, embossed grapes, Poppies, Prov Sxe Mark 19.

461. Powder Box, 4¾"d, Lady with Doves, turquoise bead work, Mark 20.

462. Bowl, 10¾″l, 8¼″w, Lady with Swallows, dark blue iridescent Tiffany finish, Mark 20.

463. Plate, 8″d, Woman Holding Roses I, pearl luster finish, Prov Sxe Mark 19.

464. Plate, 8″d, Woman Holding Roses II, pearl luster finish, Prov Sxe Mark 19.

465. Tea Set: Tea Pot, 7″h, Goddess of Fire figural scene on front, single flame on reverse side; Sugar and Creamer, 7″h, portrait decor, Mark 20.

466. Cracker Jar, 4¾″h, 8½″w, classical scene, Prov Sxe Mark 40.

467. Cup and Saucer, Queen Louise portrait, Prov Sxe
Mark 21.

468. Plate, 6½"d, classical figural scene after Angelica
Kauffmann, Prov Sxe Mark 40.

469. Match Holder, 3"x5", Napoleon portrait, Prov Sxe
Mark 20.

470. Cup, 1¾"h and Saucer, figural scene: Woman with
Letter, Mark 20.

471. Vase, 8″h, Goddess of the Sea, deep wine finish at neck and on body with heavy gold accents, Prov Sxe Mark 20.

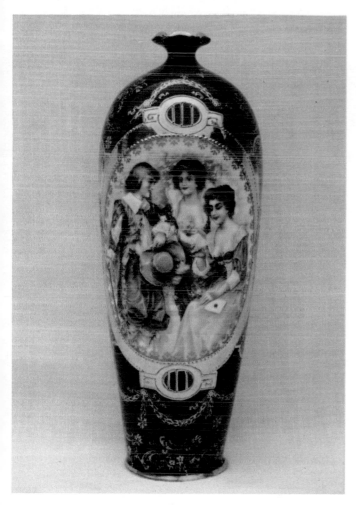

472. Vase, 9¼"h, figural scene: Woman with Letter, Mark 20.

473. Vase, 10¾"h, Lady with Swallows, lavender iridescent finish Prov Sxe Mark 19.

474. Vase, 7"h, Lady with Doves, pearl luster finish, Mark 19.

475. Vase, 3½"h (salesman's sample), Lady with Peacock, turquoise beading, iridescent blue-green Tiffany finish at top, Mark 20.

476. Vase, 12¼″h, Goddess of the Sea, floral designs outlined in gold, pearl luster finish.

477. Vase, 8½"h, handles pierced at base, Goddess of the Sea, pearl luster finish, Mark 20.

478. Vase, 6½"h, Lady with Swallows, pearl luster finish, Mark 20.

480. Vase, 8¾"h, figural portraits on four sides: front, Lady with Peacock, Mark 20.

479. Vase, 7½"h, figural portrait: Woman Holding Flowers, enamelled background, Mark 20.

481. Vase, 5"h, three handles, Lady with Doves, turquoise beading on body, Mark 20.

482. Ewer, 10"h, Lady with Swallows, Mark 20.

483. Ewer, 7¼"h, portrait decor on four sides: front, Lady with Peacock, Mark 20.

484. Vase, 11¼"h, figural portrait: Woman Holding Flowers, Mark 20.

485. Vase, 7½″h, Chickens and Daisies, Mark 20.

486. Vase, 11″h, Cattle scene, Mark 20.

487. Vase, 11¼"h, figural portrait: Woman Holding Flowers, Mark 20.

488. Vase, 11½"h, Goddess of the Sea, Mark 20.

489. Vase, 14″h, unusual design with three handles at base, figural portraits on four sides: front, Lady with Doves, Mark 20.

490. Vase, 10¾"h, two pierced handles on lower half of vase, Lady with Peacock, pearl luster finish, Mark 20.

491. Vase, 9¾″h, Woman Holding Roses I, pink and yellow enamelled flowers, Prov Sxe Mark 19.

492. Vase, 8″h, Woman Holding Roses II, pink and yellow enamelled flowers, Mark 19.

493. Covered Urn, 11¼″h, figural scene after Kauffmann, pearl luster finish, Mark 20.

494. Vase, 3″h, salesman's sample in original box, Lady with Peacock, Mark 20.

495. Relish, 8″x6½″, tapestry body finish overall, Windmill scene, Prov Sxe Mark 21.

496. Celery, 12″l, tapestry body finish overall, Windmill scene, Mark 21.

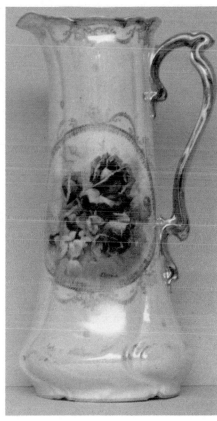

498. Tankard, 15″h, Roses, pearl luster finish, Mark 20.

497. Pair of Candle Holders, 4¾″h, floral decor, Mark 20.

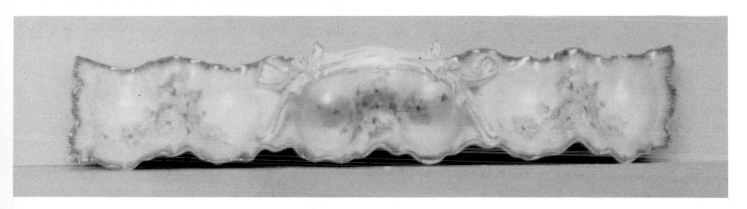

499. Egg Dish, handled, pastel flowers, gold trim Mark 20.

171

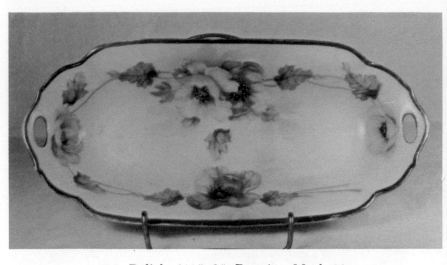

500. Tray, 11¼″x8″, Poppies, Mark 20.

501. Relish, 3½″x8″, Poppies, Mark 20.

502. Bowl, 4″ sq, handles, pink and white flowers, enamelled, Mark 20.

503. Relish, 7½″ sq, 4 leaf Clover shape with handle, pink and white flowers, Mark 20.

504. Bowl, 10½″d, yellow and red Roses, Mark 20.

505. Cake Plate, 10½″d, Gibson Girl portrait, Mark 20.

506. Chocolate Set: Chocolate Pot, 9"h, Cups, 4"h, Mums, Mark 20.

507. Chamberstick, 3"h, 6"l, Snowballs, gold trim, unmarked.

508. Tea Strainer, 6"d, floral garlands, Mark 20.

509. Child's Tea Set for six: Teapot, Creamer and Sugar, 2 Cake Plates, 6 Plates, 6 Cups and Saucers, Roses, Mark 20.

510. Bowl, 8½"d, scenic Bird decor, Mark 20.

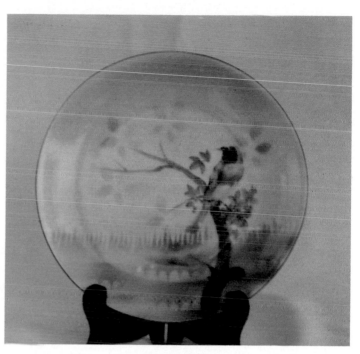

511. Plate, 6"d, Bird on Branch, Mark 20.

512. Plate, 6"d, Bird on Branch, Mark 20.

513. Plate, 6"d, Bird on Branch, Mark 20.

514. Bowl, 10¼"d, pink and white Roses, ES Thuringia, Mark 39.

515. Salt and Pepper Shakers, 3"h, Roses, ES Script Mark 17.

516. Cuspidor, 5"h, 7¾"d, marked "Erdmann Schlegelmilch, Suhl, Prussia."

517. Sugar and Creamer, 4"h, Poppies, marked "Erdmann Schlegelmilch, Thuringia, Handpainted," in green (mark not shown).

518. Tea Pot, 4"h, Poppies, same ES mark as #517.

519. Plate, 9″d, Roses, gold trim, ES monogram, Mark 41.

520. Plate, 8½″d, multicolored Roses, Mark 41.

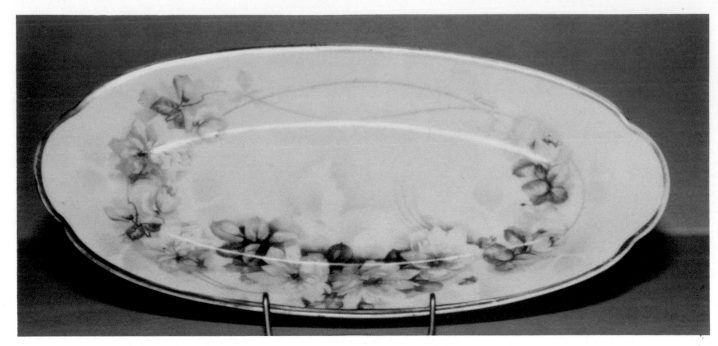

521. Celery, 12″x5½″, mixed flowers, Bird Mark 18 with "Handpainted."

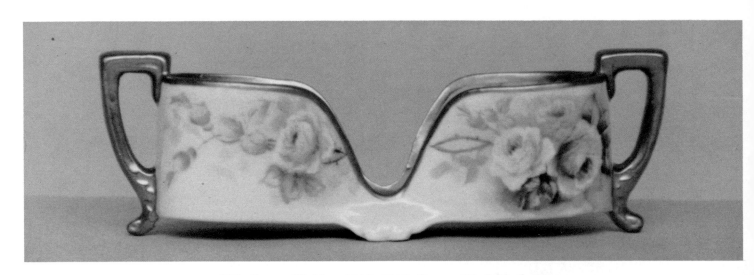

522. Spoon Holder, 7¾″x2½″, Roses, Bird Mark 18.

523. Plate, 6″d, yellow Roses, Bird Mark 18.

524. Plate, 8½″d, pink Roses, artist signature "Bernay," Bird Mark 18 with "Handpainted."

9. Reinhold Schlegelmilch's Other RS Marked Porcelain (Photographs 525 to 656)

525. Berry Dishes, 5½"d (Master Bowl not shown), mixed floral spray, embossed work around outer border, RS Wing mark, Mark 49.

526. Toothbrush Holder, 4½"x3", violets, gold trim, note three sided shade, RS Wing mark, Mark 49.

527. Spooner, 5"x6", footed, pierced work at base, floral decor, Steeple Mark 1.

528. Toothpick Holder, 2¼"h, footed, pierced work at base, floral decor, Steeple Mark 3.

529. Relish, 9½"l, floral mold, gold leaves and outlining, Steeple Mark 1.

530. Nut Dish, 3¼"x6", 3 feet, floral mold, five sided, Mixed Flowers, Steeple Mark 3.

532. Celery, 13½"x6" (RSP Mold 51 in Book I), Roses, Steeple Mark 3.

531. Sugar and Creamer, 4½"h, (RSP Mold 576 in Book I), Roses, Steeple Mark 42.

533. Plate, 8¼″d, leaf border mold, figural scene of semi-nude Woman, iridescent blue-green inner border, Steeple Mark 3.

534. Plate, 8¼″d, mythological figural scene of Woman with Wings, iridescent red inner border, Steeple Mark 3.

535. Cake Plate, 11½"d, Mixed Flowers, heavy gold border, Steeple Mark 3.

536. Bowl, 10¼"d, fancy irregular scalloped border, Lady Watering Flowers scenic decor, unmarked.

537. Bowl, 10"d, heavily embossed berries and scroll designs on border, three medallion reserves decorated with cameo figurals: Lady with Fan, Lady with Dog, Lady Watering Flowers, unmarked.

538. Butter Dish with liner, multicolored flowers, heavy gold borders, Steeple Mark 3.

539. Tankard, 11½″h (similar to RSP Mold 520), Mixed Flowers, iridescent Tiffany finish at top, Steeple Mark 3.

540. Plate, 10½"d, open handles, irregular scrolled border mold, Cobalt Blue decor on white with gold outlining and trim, Steeple Mark 2.

541. Vase, 5¼"h, Cobalt Blue decor on white, flowers and grasses, gold accents, Steeple Mark 1.

542. Cake Plate, 10¼"d, Queen Louise portrait, Steeple Mark 1.

543. Gravy, 3″x6½″ with attached Underplate, (RSP Mold 26), Steeple Mark 3.

544. Leaf Dish, 10¼″d, Steeple Mark 42.

545. Bowl, 10″d, multicolored flowers, Steeple Mark 3.

546. Berry Bowl, 7½″d, molded flowers around border, Roses, Steeple Mark 42.

547. Toothpick Holder, 2½″h, Tulips, Steeple Mark 3.

548. Candle Holder, 4½″h, Courting figural scene on base, Steeple Mark 2.

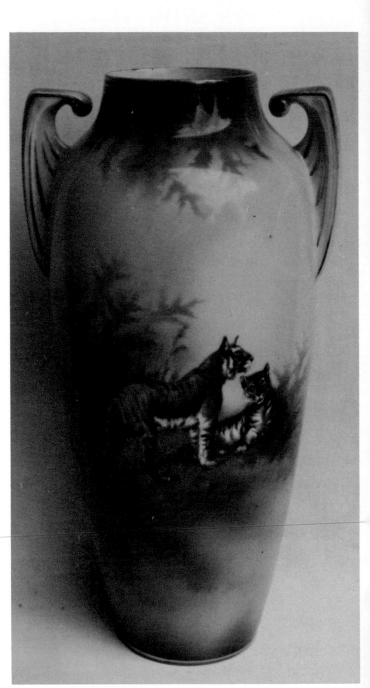

549. Vase, 12″h, Lions (rare Jungle Animal theme), unmarked. Note that Mold is usually found with R.S. Suhl or R.S. Poland marks.

550. Vase, 12″h, Tigers, unmarked.

551. Vase, 11″h, Farm Scene with Man and Cow in foreground, unmarked.

552. Vase, 9½″h, Gibson Girl portrait, R.S. Suhl, Mark 16.

553. Vase, 8″h, Cavaliers figural decor based on Rembrandt's Night Watch painting, R.S. Suhl, Mark 16.

554. Vase, 6″h, Night Watch figural scene after Rembrandt, R.S. Suhl, Mark 47.

555. Vase, 7½"h, Melon Eaters, R.S. Suhl plus "Melonenesser v. Murillo" marked on base, Mark 16.

556. Vase, 9½"h, mythological figural scene after Kauffmann, R.S. Suhl, Mark 16.

557. Tazza, 2½″x4¼″, Roses, gold stencilled designs, R.S. Suhl, Mark 47.

558. Bowl, 10″d, three leaf Clover embossed on border, Sheepherder scenic decor, R.S. Suhl, Mark 16.

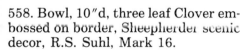

559. Inkwell and Pen Tray, 9″x6″, bold Rose and Leaf decor overall, R.S. Suhl, Mark 47.

560. Lettuce Bowl, 9″d (RSP Mold 12), Iris, pearl luster finish, RS Germany Mark 25.

561. Bowl, 11″d (RSP Mold 205), white flowers with red berries, RS Germany Mark 26.

562. Plate, 6½″d (RSP Mold 182), Poppies, pearl luster finish, RS Germany Mark 26.

563. Plate, 6¼″d (RSP Mold 205), Asters, RS Germany Mark 27 (in orange).

564. Bowl, 9½″d, (RSP Mold 336), Scattered Flowers, RS Germany Mark 48.

565. Bowl, 11″d (RSP Mold 252), mixed white flowers, RS Germany Mark 26.

566. Bowl, 9½″d (RSP Mold 151), white flowers, RS Germany Mark 25.

567. Bowl, 7″d, open work on each side, Roses, RS Germany Mark 25.

568. Plate, 10″d, pierced handles, Roses, RS Germany Mark 26.

569. Bowl, 7″d, double pierced handles, marbled orange and white finish, RS Germany Mark 26.

570. Tray, 11½″x7″ (RSP Mold 428), Fruit theme: pear, plums, strawberries, RS Germany Mark 25 in gold.

571. Bowl, 11″d, Medieval House scene, RS Germany Mark 25.

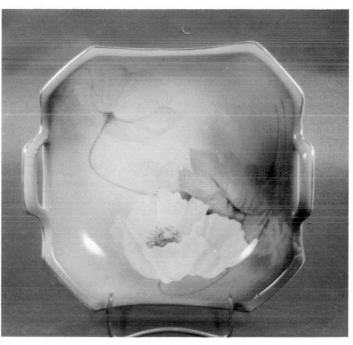

572. Bowl, 6⅛"d, pierced handles, white stylized flowers, RS Germany Mark 25 with "Handpainted" in gold.

573. Square Bowl in Art Deco style, RS Germany Mark 26.

574. Plate 8"d, 3 handles, Snowballs, RS Germany Mark 25.

575. Bowl, 7¼"d, pierced on 3 sides, multicolored flowers, RS Germany Mark 25.

576. Plate, 8″d, Bird of Paradise, RS Germany Mark 25.

577. Plate, 8″d, Flamingoes and Roses, RS Germany Mark 24.

579. Relish, 6½″l, double pierced handles, Bird of Paradise, RS Germany Mark 25.

578. Plate, 8″d, Parrots, RS Germany Mark 25.

580. Plate, 8″d, white flowers, gold stencilled designs, RS Germany Mark 25.

581. Plate, 10½″d, Tulips with gold leaves in Art Nouveau style, RS Germany Mark 24.

582. Celery, 10″x4″, Poppies, RS Germany Mark 25.

583. Plate, 8″d, Poppies, RS Germany Mark 27.

584. Cake Plate, 11″d, mixed flowers, RS Germany Mark 25.

585. Dessert Plate, 7″d, stylized floral decor, RS Germany Mark 24.

586. Plate, 6½″d, Horse Chestnut, RS Germany Mark 25.

587. Plate, 8¼″d, Cotton Boll, RS Germany Mark 24.

588. Chocolate Set: Chocolate Pot, 9″h, 2 Cups and Saucers, handpainted blank Art Deco geometric decor, RS Germany Mark 25.

589. Chocolate Set: Chocolate Pot, 10″h, Cups, 3″h, Tulips, RS Germany Mark 25.

591. Chocolate Set: Chocolate Pot with 6 Cups and Saucers, Snowballs, RS Germany Mark 25.

590. Coffee Pot, Creamer, Sugar, and Tray, cameos of small birds, Tree Roses, matte green body finish, RS Germany Mark 26.

592. Clown Figural Milk Pitcher, unmarked. (This item is seen with RS Germany Mark 25.)

593. Coffee Pot, 11"h, Roses, RS Germany Mark 25.

594. Coffee Pot, 10"h (RSP Mold 606 in Book I), Roses, RS Germany Mark 26.

595. Chocolate Pot, 6"h; Coffee Pot, 10½"h, white and apricot flowers, RS Germany Mark 26.

596. Lemonade or Milk Pitcher, 6″x9″, Roses, RS Germany Mark 26.

597. Sugar, 5″h, Calla Lily, RS Germany Mark 25.

599. Chocolate Set: Chocolate Pot 10″h, 2 cups and Saucers (RSP Mold 463, Sunflower Mold), RS Germany Mark 25.

598. Cracker Jar, 6½″x8″, Poppies, RS Germany Mark 25.

600. Individual Coffee Pot, 5½″h, RS Germany Mark 25.

601. Creamer, 4″h, Magnolias, RS Germany Mark 26.

602. Creamer, 3½″h, mixed flowers, RS Germany Mark 26.

603. Chocolate Pot, 9″h, Poppies, RS Germany Mark 27.

604. Syrup, 3″h, Roses, gold stencilled designs, RS Germany Mark 25.

605. Syrup, 3″h, Roses, gold trim, RS Germany Mark 25.

606. Salt and Pepper Shakers and Vinegar Cruet, Roses, RS Germany Mark 25.

607. Condiment Set: Salt and Pepper Shakers, Mustard Pot, Tray, Mums, RS Germany Mark 26.

608. Mayonnaise Dish and Ladle, floral decor, RS Germany Mark 26.

609. Compote, stylized white flowers, RS Germany Mark 24.

610. Cheese Server, Roses, RS Germany Mark 25.

611. Mayonnaise Dish, 4″d with Ladle and Underplate, 5½″d, Snowballs, RS Germany Mark 25.

612. Nut Set (RSP Mold 557), RS Germany Mark 27.

613. Nut Dish, 6½″d, Medieval House scene, RS Germany Mark 25.

614. Napkin Ring, floral decor, gold trim, RS Germany Mark 26.

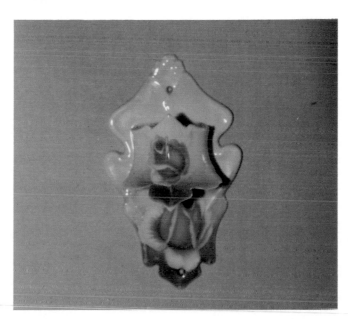

615. Match Holder, Roses, pearl luster finish, RS Germany Mark 25.

616. Relish, 10″l, stylized white flowers, RS Germany Mark 26.

617. Basket, Robin on Tree Branch, RS Germany Mark 25.

618. Ash Tray, Roses, RS Germany Mark 25.

619. Mustard Pot, 3½″h with Ladle, Lily of the Valley, RS Germany Mark 25.

620. Berry Set: Master Bowl, 9″d; Individual Bowls, 4½″d; Lilies, RS Germany Mark 26.

621. Mustard Pot, 2″hx4½″l, Ladle and Underplate, Roses, RS Germany Mark 27.

622. Dresser Set: Tray, Pair of Candle Holders, 2 Covered Boxes, silver floral decor, handpainted blanks, RS Germany Mark 25.

623. Dresser Set: Tray, Hair Receiver, Powder Box, Snowballs, RS Germany Mark 28.

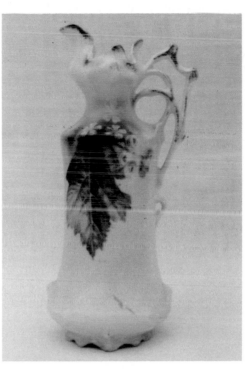

626. Bud Vase, 6″h, Roses, RS Germany Mark 27.

624. Talcum Shaker, Tulips, RS Germany Mark 25.

625. Ewer, 5½″h, large leaf with white flowers, RS Germany Mark 27.

627. Vase, 4″h (RSP Mold 909), Salesman's sample Windmill scene, RS Germany Mark 27.

628. Vase (RSP Mold 909), 4½″h, Salesman's sample, Lady Watering Flowers, RS Germany Mark 25.

629. Cologne Bottle, Butterfly and Flowers, Turquoise trim, RS Germany Mark 25.

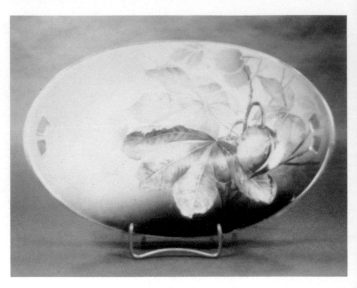

630. Oval Bowl, 10″x6¾″, Pheasants, R.S. Tillowitz without Silesia, Mark 30.

631. Oval Plate, 13″x8″, Horse Chestnuts, Mark 30 in green.

633. Cake Plate, Demi-tasse Cup and Saucer, Syrup, Gravy, and Celery, white flowers, R.S. Tillowitz, Silesia, Mark 30.

632. Vase, 10¾″h, Peace Bringing Plenty, R.S. Silesia, Mark 32.

634. Milk Pitcher, 8½"h, pink floral garland around neck, R.S. Tillowitz, Silesia, Mark 30.

635. Syrup, 4"h, white flowers, Mark 30 (without Handpainted).

636. Plate, 6¾" sq, floral decor in Art Deco style, Mark 31 with "Royal" (Royal R.S. Silesia).

637. Plate, 7"d, handles, stylized Butterfly border, R.S. Tillowitz, Silesia, Mark 30.

638. Sugar (RSP Mold 704), 4½″h, Roses, R.S. Poland, Mark 34.

639. Creamer (RSP Mold 704), 4½″h, Violets, R.S. Poland, Mark 34.

640. Tray, 14″x5″, Bird on floral branch, R.S. Poland, Mark 34.

641. Dresser Set: Chamber Stick, Tray, Hatpin Holder, 2 Pin Boxes, mythological figural scenes, R.S. Poland, Mark 33.

642. Jardiniere, 3½″h, Salesman's sample, Roses, satin finish, R.S. Poland, Mark 33.

643. Flower Holder with attached metal frog, 7″h, Pheasants, R.S. Poland, Mark 33.

644. Vase, 9″h, Farm Scene with Man and Cow in foreground, R.S. Poland, Mark 34.

645. Vase, 13″h, white and brown Pheasants, R.S. Poland, Mark 34.

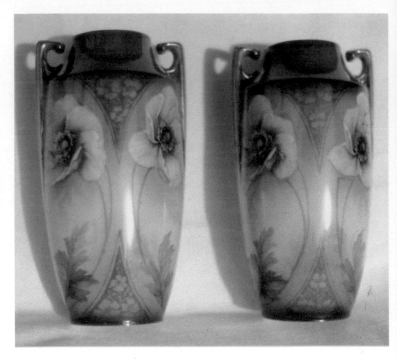

646. Hatpin Holder, 4¾"h, Crowned Cranes, R.S. Poland, Mark 33.

647. Vase, 4"h (RSP Mold 909), House by Lake scenic decor, Salesman's sample, R.S. Poland, Mark 34.

648. Pair of Vases, 7"h (R.S. Suhl Mold), stylized Poppies, R.S. Poland, Mark 34.

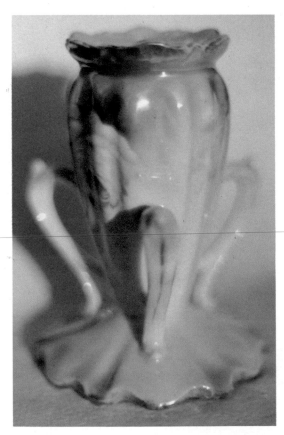

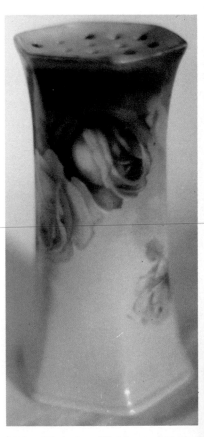

649. Talcum Shaker, three handles, Roses, R.S. Poland, Mark 34.

650. Hatpin Holder, 4½"h (RSG Mold, see Photo 543 in Book I), white Roses, Mark 53 without RS Germany (only Friedrich II in green).

651. Hatpin Holder, 4½"h, Roses, Mark 53 without RS Germany.

652. Bowl, 5″ sq, Tulips, Mark 53 (Friedrich II only).

654. Pair of Vases, 4½″h, Roses, Salesman's sample, Mark 53 (Friedrich II only).

653. Plate, 7½″d, white flowers, Mark 53 (Friedrich II only).

655. Plate, 12″d, pierced handles, stylized Poppies, Mark 53 (Friedrich II only).

656. Plate, 8½″d, stylized Roses, Mark 53 (Friedrich II only).

10. Oscar Schlegelmilch's OS Marked Porcelain
(Photographs 657 to 674)

657. Plate, 7½"d, portrait decor, "Longoire" transfer signature, OS Mark 54.

658. Tray, 10"x7", mythological scenic decor, "Boucher" transfer signature, OS Mark 54.

659. Plate, 9½"d, deep wine border with Jewels decorated as rubies, mythological scene, OS Mark 54.

660. Bowl, 10"d, classical figural scene after Kauffmann, OS Mark 55.

661. Cracker Jar, 6″x9½″, classical figural scene, OS Mark 54.

662. Cup, 1¾″h, classical scene; Saucer, 4½″d, floral reserves, OS Mark 54.

663. Plate, 11½″d, figural scene: two semi-nude women with rabbit and bird on a stick, OS Mark 54.

664. Plate, 9″d, The Gleaners figural and scenic decor based on the painting by Millet, OS Mark 54.

665. Creamer, 4½″x6″, mythological Bathing scene, OS Mark 54.

666. Butter Set: Butter Plate, 6½″d; Butter Pats (4), 3¼″d, mixed flowers, gold luster trim, OS Mark 56.

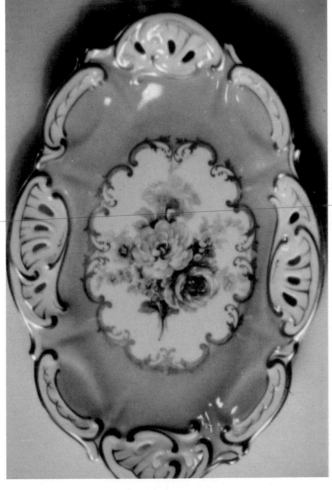

667. Oval Bowl, pierced border, floral decor, OS mark of a Crown and the initial "L" (mark not shown).

668. Tea Pot, 6½″h, fruit decor, gold luster trim, OS Mark 54.

669. Tankard, 14½"h, mythological scene, OS Mark 54.

670. Muffineer, 5"h, mythological scene, OS Mark 54.

671. Berry Drainer and Underplate, mythological scene, OS Mark 54.

672. Divided Dish with center handle, 9¾"x9" overall, Stag decor, OS Mark 54.

673. Bowl, 10½″d, Monk with Wine Glass, OS Mark 54.

674. Berry Set: Master Bowl, 10½″d; Individual Bowls (6), 5″d, Monk filling ale cup, OS Mark 54.

Bibliography

Ananoff, Alexandre, *L'oeuvre Dessiné* de Francois Boucher. Paris: F. De Nobele, Librarie, 1966.

Barber, Edwin Atlee, *The Ceramic Collectors' Glossary.* New York: Da Capo Press, 1967.

Barlock, George E. and Eileen. *The Treasures of R. S. Prussia,* 1976.

Bartran, Margaret. *A Guide to Color Reproductions.* Second edition. Metuchen, New Jersey: The Scarcecrow Press, Inc., 1971.

Bearne, Mrs. *A Court Painter and His Circle, Francois Boucher.* London: Adelphi Terrace, 1913.

Benson, E. F. *The White Eagle of Poland.* New York: George H. Doran Company, n.d.

Boger, Louise Ade. *The Dictionary of World Pottery and Porcelain.* New York: Charles Scribner's Sons, 1971.

Buell, Raymond Leslie. *Poland: Key to Europe.* London: Jonathan Cape, 1939.

Calvert, Albert F. (ed.). *Murillo: The Spanish Series.* London: John Lane, The Bodley Head Gallery, MCMVII.

Castries, Duc de. *Madame Récamier.* Hachette, 1971.

Catalogue of Reproductions of Paintings Prior to 1860. Paris: UNESCO, 1972.

Chaffers, William. *Handbook of Marks and Monograms on Pottery and Porcelain.* Revised edition. London: William Reeves, 1968.

_____.*Marks & Monograms on Pottery and Porcelain.* Vol. 1, 15th Revised edition. London: William Reeves, 1965.

Chroscicki, Leon. *Porcelana — Znaki Wytworni Europejskich.* Warszawa: Wybawnictwo Artystyczno-Graficzne, 1974.

Cox, W. E. *The Book of Pottery and Porcelain.* Vol. 1. New York: L. Lee Shepard Co., Inc., 1944.

Cushion, J.P. *Pocket Book of German Ceramic Marks and Those of Other Central European Countries.* London: Faber and Faber, 1961.

Cushion, J. P. (in collaboration with W. B. Honey). *Handbook of Pottery and Porcelain Marks.* London: Faber & Faber, 1956.

Danckert, Ludwig. *Handbuch des Europäischen Porzellans.* Munchen: Prestel-Verlag, 1954 & 1978.

Day, William E. *Blue Book of Art Values.* Third edition. Paducah, Kentucky: Collector Books, 1979.

Dyboski, Roman. *Outlines of Polish History.* London: George Allen & Unwin, Ltd. Revised edition, 1931.

Encyclopedia Britannica, Inc. Vol. 18. Chicago: William Benton, 1970.

Fayard, Artheme (ed.). *Souvenirs De Mme. Louise Elisabeth Vigee-LeBrun.* Paris: F. Funch-Bretana.

Gaston, Mary Frank. *The Collector's Encyclopedia of Limoges Porcelain.* Paducah, Kentucky: Collector Books, 1980.

_____. *The Collector's Encyclopedia of R. S. Prussia.* Paducah, Kentucky: Collector Books, 1982.

_____. "Rare R. S. (Schlegelmilch) Marks." *Schroeder's Insider,* December, 1983.

_____ . "More Schlegelmilch Marks!" *Schroeder's Insider,* October, 1984.

Graul, Richard and Albrecht Kurzwelly. *Alt Thuringer Porzellan,* 1909.

Haggar, Reginald G. *The Concise Encyclopedia of Continental Pottery and Porcelain.* New York: Hawthorne Books, Inc., 1960.

Hall, James. *Dictionary of Subjects and Symbols in Art.* Revised edition. New York: Harper & Row, 1979.

Hammond, Dorothy. *Confusing Collectibles.* Des Moines, Iowa: Wallace Homestead, 1969.

Honey, W. B. *German Porcelain.* London: Faber and Faber, MCMXLVII.

Hyamson, Albert M. *A Dictionary of Universal Biography of all Ages and of all People.* Second edition. New York: E. P. Dutton & Co., Inc. 1951.

LaRousse Encyclopedia of World Georgraphy. New York: Odyssey Press. Adapted from *Geographie Universelle Larousse.* Western Publishing Co., 1965.

Lehner, Lois. *Complete Book of American Kitchen and Dinnerware.* Des Moines:Wallace-Homestead, 1980.

Leistikow-Duchardt, Annelore. *Die Entwicklung eines neuen Stiles im Porzellan.* Heidelberg: Carl Winter Universitatsverlag, 1957.

Lewis, C. T. Courtney. *The Picture Printer of the Nineteenth Century: George Baxter.* London: Sampson Low, Marsten & Co., Ltd. 1911.

Lucas, E. V. *Chardin and Vigee-Lebrun.* London: Methuen & Co., Ltd., n.d.

Meyers Grosses Konversations-Lexikon. 6th ed. Vol. 17. Leipzig and Vienna: Biblographisches Institut, 1907.

Mountfield, David. *The Antique Collectors' Illustrated Dictionary.* London: Hamlyn, 1974.

Muehsam, Gerd (ed.). *French Painters and Paintings from the Fourteenth Century to Post Impressionism.* New York: Frederich Ungar Publishing Co., 1970.

Norman, Geraldine. *Nineteenth-Century Painters and Painting: A Dictionary.* Thames and Hudson, 1977.

Penkala, Maria. *European Porcelain A Handbook for the Collector.* Second edition. Rutland, Vermont: Charles E. Tuttle, 1968.

Poche, Emanuel. *Porcelain Marks of the World.* New York: Arco Publishing Co., Inc., 1974.

Röntgen, Robert E. *Marks on German, Bohemian and Austrian Porcelain: 1710 to the Present.* Exton, Pennsylvania: Schiffer Publishing Co., 1981.

Rose, William John. *The Drama of Upper Silesia.* Brattleboro, Vermont: Stephen Daye Press, 1935.

Schlegelmilch, Clifford J. *Handbook of Erdmann and Reinhold Schlegelmilch, Prussia-Germany and Oscar Schlegelmilch, Germany.* Third edition, 1973.

Sorenson, Don C. *My Collection R. S. Prussia,* 1979.

Stryienski, Casimir (ed.). *Memoirs of the Countess Potocka.* New York: Doubleday & McClure Co., 1901.

Terrell, George W., Jr. *Collecting R. S. Prussia: Identification and Values.* Florence, Albama: Books Americana, 1982.

Thalheim, Karl G. and A. Hillen Ziegfeld (eds.). *Der deutsche Osten. Seine Geschichte, sein Wesen und seine Aufgabe.* Berlin: Propylaen, 1936.

The Antique Trader Price Guide to Antiques. Dubuque, Iowa: Babka Publishing Company, Inc., Summer 1979, Volume X, No. 2, Issue No.32.

The Ceramist. Vol. 3 Winter Quarter, 1923.

The International Geographic Encyclopedia and Atlas. Boston: Houghton Mifflin Company, 1979.

The World Book Atlas. Field Enterprises Educational Corporation, 1973.

Thorne, J. O. (ed). *Chambers Biographical Dictionary.* Revised edition. New York: St. Martin's Press, 1969.

Treharne, R. F. and Harold Fullard (eds.). *Muir's Historical Atlas Medieval and Modern.* Tenth edition. New York: Barnes and Noble, Inc. 1964.

Wandycz, Piotr S. *The Lands of Partitioned Poland, 1795-1918.* Seattle: University of Washington Press, 1923.

Webster's Biographical Dictionary. Springfield, Mass.: G. and C. Merriam Company, 1976.

Webster's New Geographical Dictionary. Springfield, Mass.; G. and C. Merriam Company, 1972.

Weis, Gustav. *Ullstein Porzellanbuch.* Frankfurt, Berlin, Wein: Verlag Ullstein Gimblt, 1975. First edition, 1964.

Index to Objects

Ash Tray—618
Baskets—213, 351, 617
Berry Drainer—671
Berry Sets—43, 64, 77, 95, 107, 114, 140, 620, 674
Bowls—1-5, 8, 13, 14, 25-27, 29, 30, 34-36, 41, 42, 45, 46, 51, 53, 56-59, 61-63, 65-67, 69, 71, 74, 75, 78, 82, 83, 85, 87-93, 90-102, 104, 105, 108, 109, 111, 113, 115, 121, 124-127, 129-131, 133-136, 138, 146, 147, 151, 159, 160, 162-166, 178, 179, 181, 182, 184-187, 458-460, 462, 502, 504, 510, 514, 525, 536, 537, 545, 546, 558, 561, 564-567, 569, 571-573, 575, 630, 652, 660, 667, 672, 673
Bun Trays—23, 80, 176
Butter Dish—538
Butter Set—666
Cabbage Bowl—20
Cake Plates—6, 9, 11, 16, 39, 40, 44, 50, 54, 55, 60, 68, 103, 119, 122, 128, 132, 137, 139, 142, 144, 145, 148, 152, 156, 167, 172, 173, 175, 290, 505, 535, 542, 584, 633
Candle Holders—393, 497, 548, 622
Celery Dishes—48, 94, 123, 142, 149, 150, 154, 174, 180, 183, 496, 521, 532, 582, 633
Centerpiece Bowls—106, 214, 222, 313
Chambersticks—451, 452, 507, 641
Cheese Server—610
Children's Dishes—289, 509
Chocolate Pots—190, 192, 237, 241, 255, 290, 323, 326, 330, 348, 595, 603
Chocolate Sets—212, 229, 230, 260, 285, 287, 288, 340, 355, 363, 445, 506, 588, 589, 591, 599
Coffee Pots (also see Demi-tasse Pots) 339, 590, 593-595, 600
Coffee Set—317
Cognac Bottle—442
Cologne Bottle—629
Compotes—168, 609
Cracker Jars—208, 217, 228, 231, 234, 239, 252, 263, 266, 270, 276, 279, 320, 322, 328, 332, 336, 343, 354, 439, 466, 598, 661
Cream Soup Cup—309
Creamers—254, 268, 272, 292, 311, 314, 318, 353, 601, 602, 639, 665
Cups (also see Chocolate Pots, Chocolate Sets, Coffee Pots, Tea Sets)—210, 235, 264, 265, 310, 319, 345
Cup and Saucers—195, 290, 359, 467, 470, 662
Cuspidor—516
Demi-tasse Cups—196-198, 201, 283, 346, 633
Demi-tasse Pots—204, 205, 273, 274, 331, 364
Demi-tasse Sets—203, 286
Dessert Set—11
Dresser Sets—392, 622, 623, 641
Egg Dish—499
Egg Warmer—198
Ewers—440, 448, 482, 483, 625
Ferners—400-403, 643
Footed Bowls—47, 49, 52, 70, 155, 169, 170, 367
Gravy Dish—543, 633
Hair Receivers—383-386, 623
Hatpin Holders—368-378, 641, 646, 650, 651
Inkwell—559
Jam Jars—206, 209, 233
Jardiniere—642

Leaf Dishes—14, 15, 17, 18, 544
Lemonade Pitchers—211, 257, 267, 271, 294, 340, 361, 362, 596
Letter Holders—394
Lettuce Bowls—19, 20, 560
Lobster Dish—446
Loving Cup—436
Match Holders—469, 615
Mayonnaise Dishes—608, 611
Muffineers (or Talcum Shakers)—379-382, 624, 670
Mustache Cups—327, 366
Mustard Pots—227, 243, 259, 261, 308, 335, 607, 619, 621
Napkin Ring—614
Nut Dish—530, 613
Nut Set—612
Pen Tray—559
Pin Boxes—387-391, 622, 641
Pitchers—191, 193, 236, 246, 280, 360, 441, 592, 634
Plates—12, 21, 22, 31, 33, 37, 38, 54, 72, 79, 81, 84, 86, 112, 116, 117, 132, 137, 139, 143, 153, 157, 158, 171, 188, 443, 444, 454, 455, 463, 464, 468, 511-513, 519, 520, 523, 524, 533, 534, 540, 562, 563, 568, 574, 576-578, 580, 581, 583, 585-587, 631, 636, 637, 653, 655-657, 659, 663, 664
Powder Boxes—461, 623
Receiving Card Tray—177
Relish Dishes—7, 73, 81, 113, 118, 495, 501, 503, 529, 579, 616
Salt and Pepper Shakers—278, 281, 515, 606, 607
Salt Shakers—262, 282
Shaving Mugs—235, 345, 395-399
Spoon Holder 522
Spooners—215, 216, 242, 527
Sugar Bowls—253, 269, 296, 315, 597, 638
Sugar and Creamer Sets—192, 216, 219, 232, 238, 244, 258, 275, 295, 305-307, 314, 315, 333, 340, 347, 352, 356-358, 365, 465, 517, 531
Syrup Pitchers—207, 218, 220, 221, 225, 226, 277, 284, 293, 341, 344, 604, 605, 633, 635
Talcum Shakers (also see Muffineers)—624, 649
Tankards—194, 223, 224, 240, 247-250, 297-303, 334, 338, 350, 438, 498, 539, 669
Tazza—557
Tea Pots—202, 245, 518, 668
Tea Sets—251, 291, 304, 312, 316, 324, 329, 465
Tea Strainers—200, 508
Toothbrush Holder—526
Toothpick Holders—256, 278, 321, 325, 337, 342, 349, 450, 453, 528, 547
Trays—10, 24, 28, 32, 76, 110, 120, 161, 189, 500, 570, 640, 658
Urns 437, 493
Vases—404-435, 447, 449, 456, 457, 471-481, 484-492, 494, 541, 549-556, 626-628, 632, 644, 645, 647, 648, 654
Vinegar Cruet—606

Index and Cross Reference to Popular Named Molds (Photograph Numbers)

Ball Foot (see Mold 632)—327-331, 396
Berry—55-57
Bleeding Heart—58
Cabbage (also see Lettuce)—290
Carnation—43-46, 255-257
Corduroy (see Mold 261)—137
Daisy—see Lily
Embossed Lady—see Hidden Image
Feather—see Plume
Fleur-de-lys—12, 13, 308, 432
Grape—1-3, 416
Hidden Image—4-9, 235, 236, 387
Honeycomb—59, 60
Icicle—10, 11, 194, 195, 385
Iris—39-42, 321-323
Jewel—see Ribbon and Jewel
Leaf—14-18
Lettuce—19,20
Lily—47-53
Lily of the Valley—202
Locket—61-63

Medallion—21-26, 324-326
Pie Crust—64, 354, 355
Plume—27, 193, 364
Point and Clover (see Molds 82 and 643)—79-81, 337-341
Poppy (see Carnation)
Raspberry—363
Ribbon and Jewel—28-33, 246, 399
Ripple (see Molds 259 and 861)—135, 395
Ruffle—see Stippled Floral
Sea Creature—34
Scallop and Fan (see Molds 278 and 501)—145, 210-215
Shield—65-67
Six Medallion (see Mold 78)—76, 77
Square and Jewel—35
Stippled Floral—36-38, 247-254
Strawberry—68
Sunflower—54, 318
Swag and Tassel (see Mold 155)—109, 110
Tear-Drop—69
Tulip and Ribbon—70

Index to Decoration Themes (RSP Items)

Animal:
    Stag—134
    Gazelles—168
Barnyard Animals—154, 371
Birds:
    Bird of Paradise—137, 390
    Ducks—109, 152, 297, 325
    Hummingbird—113
    Parrots—113
    Peacock—152, 408
    Pheasants—155, 383, 420
    Sand Snipe—116
    Snowbird—21, 24
    Swallows (Blue Birds)—23, 109-111, 153-155, 297, 305, 369, 394
    Swans—121, 153-155, 198, 207, 242, 275, 297, 300, 370, 407
    Turkeys—109, 153, 406, 409
Figural:
    Boy with Geese—248
    The Cage—431
    Cherubs and Cupids—159, 175, 291, 359
    Diana the Huntress—175, 324, 334
    Dice Throwers—33, 347, 405
    Flora—324, 434
    Girl Holding Letter (one of the Four Charmers)—158
    Melon Eaters—31, 347
    Peace Bringing Plenty—412
    Victorian Vignettes
        Couple with Woman Knitting—410, 418,421
        Couple with Woman in Swing I—411
        Couple with Woman in Swing II—417, 410
        Lady Feeding Chickens—37, 89
        Lady with Dog—38, 90, 413
        Lady with Fan—37, 174, 237, 436
        Lady Watering Flowers—38, 91
Floral (some popular themes):
    Calla Lily—206
    Canterbury Bells—118, 132, 294, 392
    Cotton Boll—189
    Dogwood and Pine—141, 142, 204, 260-262, 332, 380, 386, 401

Flowers in Glass Bowl—337, 340
Grape and Leaf—170
Hainging Basket I—26, 60, 67, 179, 299, 377, 398
Hanging Basket II—373
Laurel Chain—231
Lilies—123, 171, 223, 254, 268, 281 285, 353
Lily of the Valley—64, 140, 161, 202, 354, 355, 400
Magnolias—44, 76, 77, 88, 186, 190
Reflecting Poppies and Daisies—28, 35, 69, 195
Reflecting Water Lilies—10, 22, 151, 165, 194, 391
Roses and Snowballs—85, 128, 139, 192, 246, 303
Scattered Flowers—79, 80, 122, 164
Sitting Basket—187, 324
Snowballs—145, 146, 286
Surreal Dogwood—102, 174, 201, 230
Tulips—15, 103, 106
Fruit—114, 145, 249, 252, 272, 276
Portraits:
    Colonial Man—283, 414
    Four Seasons—98
        Autumn—71, 98
        Spring—98, 427
        Summer—83, 98, 247
        Winter—98, 125, 416, 428, 432
    Gibson Girl—115
    Madame Lebrun—25, 36, 238, 302, 326, 429
    Countess Potocka—25, 240, 404, 430
    Madame Récamier—25, 241
Portraits (miscellaneous)—47-49, 320
Scenic:
    Admiral Peary Arctic Scene—183, 362, 376
    Castle (or Church)—295, 345, 426
    Cottage—83, 92, 247, 301, 435
    Country House and Lake—188
    Evergreens—300, 325, 383
    Farm Scene—131, 208
    Man in the Mountain—11, 21, 24, 149, 385
    Masted Ship—30
    Mill—110, 269, 279, 368, 394
    Sheepherder I—24, 101-150
    Three Scenes—83, 153-155, 297

Index to Decoration Themes (Other R. S., E. S., and O. S. Marks)

Animal:
    Cattle—486
    Lions—549
    Stag—672
    Tigers—550
Birds:
    Bird of Paradise—576, 579
    Chickens—485
    Crowned Cranes—646
    Flamingoes—577
    Parrots—578
    Pheasants—630, 643, 645
Birds (miscellaneous)—510-513, 590, 617, 640
Butterfly—629, 637
Figural:
    Classical and Mythological—447, 466, 468, 493, 534, 556, 641, 658-663, 665, 669, 671
    The Gleaners—664
    Goddess of Fire—465
    Goddess of the Sea—458, 471, 476, 477, 488
    Lady with Doves—457, 461, 474, 481, 489
    Lady with Peacock—475, 480, 483, 490, 494
    Lady with Swallows—462, 473, 478, 482
    Melon Eaters—555
    The Night Watch—553, 554
    Peace Bringing Plenty—632
    Semi-Nude Woman—533
    Victorian Vignettes—536-538, 628

Woman Holding Flowers—459, 479, 484, 487
Woman Holding Letter—470, 472
Women Holding Roses—463, 464, 491, 492
Figurals (miscellaneous): 444, 465, 548, 592
Floral (same RSP transfers)
    Calla Lily—597
    Cotton Boll—587
    Lilies—620
    Lily of the Valley—619
    Magnolias—565, 601
    Scattered Flowers—564
    Snow Balls—507, 574, 591, 611, 623
Fruit—570, 668
Portrait:
    Gibson Girl—505, 552
    Indian—451, 453-456
    Monk—673, 674
    Napoleon—469
    Queen Louise—467, 542
    Woman with Daisy Crown—449, 450
Portrait (miscellaneous)—448, 657
Scenic:
    Country House and Lake—647
    Farm Scene—551, 644
    Medieval House—571, 613
    Sheepherder (RSG version)—558
    Windmill—495, 496, 627

Value Guide to Schlegelmilch China

The trend in R. S. Prussia prices has changed since my first book on the subject was published in 1982. For most antiques, prices tend to ebb and flow. During the early 1980s, it seemed that RSP was going to be an exception to that rule as prices continued upward. Looking back, it appears that prices actually peaked during 1981, about the time my first price guide was compiled. Generally, since 1982, RSP prices have leveled off rather than climbing consistently higher as they did during the late 1970s and early 1980s.

Several reasons account for this. First, the economic recession had an impact on antiques in general, and RSP was affected by those conditions as well. When interest rates reached double digits, some collectors turned to putting their dollars in guaranteed money markets rather than investing in antiques.

Second, because of those high interest rates as well as the large sums RSP was bringing at the time, many collections came on the market. As more RSP became available, items were less scarce. Consequently, prices began to drop or at least failed to rise.

Third, RSP had become so expensive that many dealers were unable to compete with collectors. Thus a large contingent of formerly active buyers was eliminated from the market. Greater availability of the product and fewer buyers automatically cause prices to descend or level off. The exhilarating "Prussia" mania began to slow down.

Dealers and collectors should not become overjoyed or despondent over those facts! The china still continues to bring much higher sums than older porcelains such as Meissen or Sèvres. If prices drop by several hundred dollars for most antiques, the result could be disastrous; but the same magnitude of variation will not destroy the market for R.S. Prussia. The china has become firmly established as a category of highly desirable porcelain. Although prices overall may be somewhat lower, they are not cheap! Popular decorations such as the Seasons and other portraits still command good prices. The rare decorations such as the jungle animals and three scene pieces are valued even higher.

The greatest price changes for RSP have not been for the choice items. Common types of items with floral decor such as bowls, cake plates, cracker jars, and so forth have suffered the most. The floral themes always have been lower in price because they were more plentiful. Thus, it is not surprising that those examples would be affected more by these trends.

In 1981, almost any floral decorated bowl with an RSP mark was in the $200 to $400 range, and those with fancy molds and popular finishes could cost even more. Collectors were actually paying for the "red mark" itself, regardless of the piece or its decoration. As more RSP became available, collectors became more selective. Also the prevalence of the "fake" mark and altered china with fake decal decoration caused collectors to became wary, realizing it was not wise to pay a premium for the mark alone.

The genuine red mark, of course, is not to be discounted, but unmarked pieces which can be matched to authenticated RSP marked examples are currently valued on a more equal basis. The same is true for items with R. S. Steeple, R. S. Suhl, and R. S. Poland marks. On the other hand, R. S. Germany marked china has not advanced appreciably and is still the lowest priced of all RS marks, unless the mold or decoration is identical to RSP items.

Erdmann Schlegelmilch's ES marked porcelain is higher than R.S. Germany but generally much lower than R. S. Prussia, R. S. Suhl, or R. S. Poland. One reason for this is the marks are different. In the past, collectors have been more intent on equating marks rather than china. Hence, other RS Wreath and star marks such as R. S. Suhl and R. S. Poland gained quick acceptance because they were so similar to the RSP mark. Another reason is that although many ES pieces are elegantly shaped and richly decorated, the shapes and decorations are definitely different from RSP molds and transfers. Figural and portrait subjects as well as unusual finishes are found on ES china. But they are not the same popular ones collectors find on RSP. To many collectors, the pieces are not "Prussia." In reality, much ES porcelain is equal to RSP when molds and art work are considered.

Prices for Oscar Schlegelmilch (OS) china are basically comparable to ES china. OS pieces are more scarce, and few examples surface. The similarity of decoration subjects and finishes, as well as the "non-RS" marks, also contributes to ES and OS items being considered on a fairly equal basis in the eyes of collectors.

As my first guide reflected the RSP market of the early 1980s, this guide attempts to show the value of the china in the more stable climate of the early 1990's. This value guide presents an average price range for the items illustrated. Random prices are not shown, although random prices asked and obtained from many different sources such as shops, shows, mail order, auctions, and private collectors were taken into account in developing the guide. Other important considerations such as the popularity or rarity of the decoration, the scarcity of the object, and the rarity of the mark were also examined. Details such as size variations for all items, mold designs, and even background colors are features which also affect values. Quoted prices assume pieces to be in mint condition.

I have tried to present a value range which adequately measures the numerous and divergent factors which influence prices for Schlegelmilch china. But this guide is not intended to set prices, and it should be used only as a guide. The user should be aware that prices well above and below those reported here may be asked and paid for the same or similar items. This is especially true for rarities.

Because it is sometimes difficult, especially for beginning collectors, to understand why one item differs in value from another, I have coded many of the pieces to indicate the special characteristics which contribute to that item's price range. Even with this method there will be variations within codes. That is to say that all decorations coded as "Popular" (PD) will certainly not all be in the same price range. Various portrait, scenic, and floral themes can all be classified as popular. Portraits are priced several hundred dollars higher than popular scenic designs, however, and considerably higher than popular floral decorations. The price variation between types of decoration themes and within decoration themes reflects the degree of popularity of each which is based basically on how they have been ranked by collectors.

For example, fruit themes are more scarce than portrait themes, but fruit themes are not as popular among collectors. Thus, pieces with fruit decor have a lower value than portrait items. Likewise, some of the same types of decoration themes, such as portrait, figural, or bird, may also be scarce or popular on other Schlegelmilch marked porcelain. Their value will usually not correspond with RSP pieces because RSP holds the highest status of all Schlegelmilch marked porcelain.

Scarce Decoration (SD) has been used to refer to those themes which are seen less frequently than others, although they may also be very popular. For example, the Farm scene is more scarce than the Man in the Mountain. Victorian Vignettes (Lady Watering Flowers, etc.) and Diana the Huntress are more scarce than portraits such as the Seasons, Lebrun, or Countess Potocka.

Objects such as syrup pitchers, mustard pots, and toothpick holders are popular items, but they are more scarce than other popular items such as chocolate pots and tankards. Thus, they are coded as scarce objects (SO). Although shaving mugs and mustache cups are more scarce than syrup pitchers, they are not really "rare," and therefore are coded as scarce also.

The designation of "rare" has been confined to extremely limited examples of either molds, decorations, objects, or marks. Gazelles, lions, and tigers are rare animal decorations. The RS Wing mark is rare. Certain objects such as an egg basket or a salesman's sample are rare.

Salesman's samples are a new classification. One example, a vase, is shown in its original box (see Photograph #494). Danckert's information stating that Reinhold had a sample showroom in New York substantiates the fact that samples were made by the factories. Vases and jardiniers which are 3″ to 4½″ in height would fit this classification.

Popular (P), Scarce (S), and Rare (R) are combined with one of the following letters to form each code.

B--Background (colors such as cobalt blue, red, wine)
D--Decoration (various decoration themes such as bird, floral, scenic, etc.)
M--Mold (shape of the object)
Mk--Mark (backmark on the object)
F--Finish (overglaze body finish such as satin, luster, Tiffany iridescent, tapestry, etc.)
O--Object (particular type of item)

Note that many entries have more than one code: (PD/SM/SO/RMk) indicates the piece has a popular decoration, a scarce mold, is a scarce object, and has a rare mark.

In the following two sections rare, popular, and scarce decorations are identified for both RS and other Schlegelmilch marks. I have marked with one asterisk (*) decorations not shown in this book; or if shown, the items do not have an RS mark. I have marked with two asteriks (**) decorations shown in Book I but not shown in this edition.

Key to Ranking Major Decoration Subjects with RS Marks

Rare--Animals:	Gazelles; Giraffes*; Lions; Tigers
Birds:	Bird of Paradise; Black Swan; Crowned Cranes; Hummingbird; Ostriches*; Parrots; Sand Snipe; Water (or Marsh) Bird
Scenic:	Admiral Peary Arctic scene
Figural:	Belles of Linden*; Boy with Geese; Semi-Nude Woman
Fruit:	any peeled or sliced-open fruit
Other:	three scenes on one item; all Four Seasons on one item
Popular--Portrait:	Countess Potocka; Four Seasons (Winter, Spring, Summer, Fall); Gibson Girls; Madame Lebrun; Countess Potocka; Madame Récamier
Figural:	Dice Throwers; Melon Eaters
Scenic:	Castle; Cottage; Evergreens; Man in the Mountain; Mill; Sheepherder I
Birds:	Barnyard Animals; Ducks; Peacock; Pheasants; Swallows (or Blue Birds); Swans; Turkeys
Floral:	Only a few floral subjects have been coded such as Cotton Boll; Dogwood and Pine; Hanging Basket; Lilies; and Sitting Basket. See the Decoration Index for several other identifiable patterns. Note that Poppies and Roses are the most common types of flowers found on RSP, and they are not coded.
Scarce--Animal:	Stag
Bird:	Snowbird
Portrait:	Colonial Man; Josephine*; Napoleon*; Queen Louise*; various unidentified persons
Figural:	The Cage; Cherubs or Cupids; Diana the Huntress; Flora; any of the Four Charmers*; any mythological or classical group; Nightwatch figures; Peace Bringing Plenty; any of the Victorian Vignettes (see index for list)
Scenic:	Country House and Lake: Farm scene; Masted Ship scenes; Medieval House; RSG Cottage**; RSG Man with Horses**; RSG Sheepherder; RSP Sheepherder II**; Windmills
Fruit:	any fruit decor

Key to Ranking Major ES and OS Decoration Subjects

Rare--Animal:	Cattle
Bird:	Chickens
Figural:	Goddess of Fire
Popular--Figural	Goddess of the Sea; Lady with Doves; Lady with Peacock; Lady with Swallows; any mythological or classical group; Woman Holding Flowers; Woman Holding Roses I and II; Woman Holding Letter
Portrait:	Woman with Daisy Crown
Scarce--Bird:	any bird decor
Figural:	The Gleaners
Fruit:	any fruit decor
Portrait:	Indians; Josephine*, Monks; Napoleon; Queen Louise
Scenic:	Windmill

Price Guide

R. S. Prussia Prices for Photographs 1 to 437

#	Desc	Low	High	#	Desc	Low	High	#	Desc	Low	High
#1	$	275.00-	325.00	#63	(SM/SD) $	300.00-	350.00	#128	$	150.00-	200.00
#2	$	225.00-	275.00	#64				#129	$	125.00-	175.00
#3	$	225.00-	300.00		(PD/PF) set $	700.00-	900.00	#130	(SF) $	225.00-	275.00
#4	(PM) $	325.00-	375.00	#65	$	250.00-	300.00	#131	(SD) $	700.00-	900.00
#5	(PM) $	300.00-	350.00	#66	$	225.00-	275.00	#132	$	150.00-	200.00
#6	(PM) $	350.00-	400.00	#67	(PD) $	350.00-	400.00	#133	$	150.00-	200.00
#7	(SO/PM) $	400.00-	450.00	#68	(SM/PF) $	300.00-	350.00	#134	(SD) $	250.00-	350.00
#8	(RM) $	325.00-	375.00	#69	$	275.00-	325.00	#135	(PM) $	250.00-	300.00
#9	(RM) $	325.00-	375.00	#70	(SO) $	125.00-	150.00	#136	(SM) $	150.00-	200.00
#10	(PM/PD) $	300.00-	400.00	#71	(PD)$	1,200.00-	1,400.00	#137	(RD) $	2,000.00-	2,400.00
#11				#72	$	150.00-	200.00	#138	$	200.00-	250.00
	(PM/PD) set $	800.00-	1,000.00	#73	$	175.00-	225.00	#139	$	225.00-	275.00
#12	$	150.00-	200.00	#74	(SM) $	300.00-	350.00	#140	(PD) set $	400.00-	500.00
#13	$	125.00-	175.00	#75	$	125.00-	175.00	#141	(PD) $	275.00-	325.00
#14	(SO) $	100.00-	125.00	#76	$	275.00-	325.00	#142	(PD) $	275.00-	325.00
#15	(SO) $	200.00-	250.00	#77	set $	700.00-	900.00	#143	$	100.00-	125.00
#16	$	175.00-	225.00	#78	$	225.00-	275.00	#144	$	200.00-	250.00
#17	(SO) $	175.00-	225.00	#79	(PM) $	250.00-	300.00	#145	(SD) $	400.00-	500.00
#18	(SO/PF) $	175.00-	225.00	#80	(PM) $	250.00-	300.00	#146	$	125.00-	175.00
#19	(SO) $	500.00-	600.00	#81	(PM) $	150.00-	175.00	#147	$	150.00-	200.00
#20	(SO) $	125.00-	150.00	#82	$	250.00-	300.00	#148	(PF) $	200.00-	250.00
#21	(PM/SD) $	1,400.00-	1,600.00	#83	(SM/RD) $	2,200.00-	2,600.00	#149	(PD) $	700.00-	900.00
#22	$	225.00-	275.00	#84	$	200.00-	250.00	#150	(PD) $	500.00-	600.00
#23	(PM/PD) $	500.00-	600.00	#85	$	225.00-	275.00	#151	(PM/SB) $	350.00-	450.00
#24				#86	$	125.00-	150.00	#152	(PM/PD) $	600.00-	800.00
	(PM/PO/PD) $	1,600.00-	1,800.00	#87	(SB/SF) $	325.00-	375.00	#153	(PM/RD) $	2,000.00-	2,400.00
#25	(PD/SB) $	1,600.00-	1,800.00	#88	$	300.00-	350.00	#154	(PM/RD) $	2,000.00-	2,400.00
#26	(PD) $	250.00-	300.00	#89	(SD) $	1,000.00-	1,200.00	#155	(PM/RD/SO) $	2,000.00-	2,400.00
#27	(PM) $	250.00-	300.00	#90	(SD) $	1,000.00-	1,200.00	#156	$	125.00-	175.00
#28	(PM/PO/PD) $	300.00-	350.00	#91	(SD) $	1,000.00-	1,200.00	#157	(RD) $	1,200.00-	1,400.00
#29	(PM) $	250.00-	300.00	#92	(PD/SB) $	800.00-	1,000.00	#158	(SD) $	1,400.00-	1,600.00
#30	(PM/SD) $	1,000.00-	1,200.00	#93	$	175.00-	225.00	#159	(SD) $	275.00-	325.00
#31	(PM/PD) $	1,200.00-	1,400.00	#94	$	200.00-	250.00	#160	(PF) $	225.00-	275.00
#32	(PM) $	250.00-	300.00	#95	set $	500.00-	600.00	#161	(PF) $	175.00-	225.00
#33	(PM/PD) $	1,400.00-	1,600.00	#96	(SM) $	300.00-	350.00	#162	$	175.00-	225.00
#34	(SM) $	300.00-	350.00	#97	$	250.00-	300.00	#163	(SB) $	300.00-	350.00
#35	$	250.00-	300.00	#98	(RD/SM) $	3,500.00-	4,000.00	#164	$	225.00-	275.00
#36	(PM/PD) $	800.00-	1,000.00	#99	$	225.00-	275.00	#165	(PD) $	300.00-	350.00
#37				#100	$	175.00-	225.00	#166	(SF) $	200.00-	250.00
	(PM/SD) (ea) $	150.00-	200.00	#101	(PD) $	700.00-	800.00	#167	$	175.00-	225.00
#38				#102	$	175.00-	225.00	#168	(RD/SO) $	4,000.00-	4,500.00
	(PM/SD) (ea) $	150.00-	200.00	#103	$	200.00-	250.00	#169	$	125.00-	150.00
#39	(PM/SB) $	400.00-	450.00	#104	$	30.00-	50.00	#170	(SD) $	150.00-	175.00
#40	(PM) $	300.00-	350.00	#105	$	250.00-	300.00	#171	(PD/PF) $	175.00-	225.00
#41	(PM) $	300.00-	350.00	#106	(SO) $	300.00-	350.00	#172	$	150.00-	200.00
#42	$	175.00-	225.00	#107	set $	500.00-	600.00	#173	$	125.00-	175.00
#43	(PM) set $	800.00-	1,000.00	#108	(PF) $	175.00-	225.00	#174	(SD) $	1,000.00-	1,200.00
#44	(PM) $	325.00-	375.00	#109	(PD) $	800.00-	1,000.00	#175	(SD/SF) $	1,400.00-	1,600.00
#45	(PM) $	325.00-	375.00	#110	(PD) $	800.00-	1,000.00	#176	(SB) $	350.00-	400.00
#46	(SM) $	350.00-	400.00	#111	(SM/PD) $	300.00-	350.00	#177	(SO) $	250.00-	300.00
#47				#112	(PF) $	100.00-	125.00	#178	$	200.00-	250.00
	(PM/SD/SO) $	500.00-	600.00	#113 Relish	(SD) $	800.00-	1,000.00	#179	(PD) $	250.00-	300.00
#48	(PM/SD) $	600.00-	700.00	Berry	(RD) $	400.00-	500.00	#180	$	150.00-	200.00
#49	(PM/SD/SO) $	500.00-	600.00	#114	(RD) set $	800.00-	1,000.00	#181	(SM) $	250.00-	300.00
#50	(PM) $	325.00-	375.00	#115	(PD) $	1,000.00-	1,200.00	#182	(SM) $	300.00-	350.00
#51	(PM) $	300.00-	350.00	#116	(RD) $	1,200.00-	1,400.00	#183	(RD) $	3,000.00-	4,000.00
#52	(PM/SO) $	325.00-	375.00	#117	$	125.00-	175.00	#184	(PF) $	250.00-	300.00
#53	(PF) $	225.00-	275.00	#118	$	150.00-	200.00	#185	(SM/SF) $	425.00-	475.00
#54	(PM) $	275.00-	325.00	#119	$	150.00-	200.00	#186	$	175.00-	225.00
#55	$	175.00-	225.00	#120	$	175.00-	225.00	#187	(PD) $	250.00-	300.00
#56	$	175.00-	225.00	#121	(PD) $	550.00-	650.00	#188	(SD) $	800.00-	1,000.00
#57	(SM) $	250.00-	300.00	#122	$	175.00-	225.00	#189	(SD) $	300.00-	350.00
#58	$	225.00-	275.00	#123	$	125.00-	175.00	#190	$	450.00-	550.00
#59	$	225.00-	275.00	#124	$	200.00-	250.00	#191	$	400.00-	500.00
#60	(PD) $	300.00-	350.00	#125	(PD) $	1,400.00-	1,600.00	#192			
#61	(SM/PF) $	250.00-	300.00	#126	$	225.00-	275.00		Chocolate Pot $	450.00-	550.00
#62	(SM/PF) $	250.00-	300.00	#127	(PF) $	150.00-	200.00		C & S set $	225.00-	275.00

#193 ....(PM) $	350.00-	450.00
#194 ....(PM) $	550.00-	650.00
#195 ....(PM) $	100.00-	125.00
#196 ....$	75.00-	100.00
#197 ....(SM) $	100.00-	125.00
#198................(RD) $	350.00-	400.00
#199 ....(SO) $	175.00-	225.00
#200 ....(SO) $	250.00-	300.00
#201 ....$	40.00-	60.00
#202 ....(RM) $	350.00-	400.00
#203 Coffee Pot $	600.00-	700.00
Cup/Saucer $	100.00-	125.00
#204 ....(PD) $	700.00-	800.00
#205 ....$	600.00-	700.00
#206 ....(SO) $	175.00-	225.00
#207 ....(PD/SO) $	350.00-	450.00
#208 ....(SD) $	800.00-	1,000.00
#209 ....(SO) $	175.00-	225.00
#210 ....(PM) $	50.00-	75.00
#211 ....(PM) $	250.00-	300.00
#212 Chocolate Pot..$	550.00-	650.00
Cup/Saucer .....$	100.00-	125.00
#213 ....(PM/RO) $	600.00-	700.00
#214 ....(PM/SO) $	350.00-	400.00
#215 ....(PM/SO) $	200.00-	250.00
#216 C & S ....set $	225.00-	275.00
Spooner...........$	150.00-	200.00
#217 ....$	275.00-	325.00
#218 ....(SO) $	200.00-	250.00
#219..................set $	200.00-	250.00
#220 ....(SO) $	250.00-	300.00
#221 ....(SO) $	250.00-	300.00
#222 ....(SO) $	325.00-	375.00
#223 ....(PD) $	550.00-	650.00
#224 ....(PM) $	550.00-	650.00
#225 ....(SO) $	250.00-	300.00
#226 ....(SO) $	250.00-	300.00
#227 ....(SO) $	175.00-	225.00
#228 ....$	250.00-	300.00
#229 Chocolate Pot..$	550.00-	650.00
Cup/Saucer .....$	75.00-	100.00
#230 Chocolate Pot..$	550.00-	650.00
Cup/Saucer ....$	75.00-	100.00
#231 ....$	225.00-	275.00
#232..................set $	200.00-	250.00
#233 ....(PF) $	275.00-	325.00
#234 ....$	250.00-	300.00
#235 ....(PM/SO) $	250.00-	300.00
#236 ....(PM) $	300.00-	350.00
#237 ....(SD) $	700.00-	900.00
#238 ....(PD) set $	1,200.00-	1,400.00
#239 ....$	275.00-	325.00
#240 ....(PD) $	1,200.00-	1,400.00
#241 ....(PD/SF) $	1,200.00-	1,400.00
#242 ....(PD/SO) $	250.00-	300.00
#243 ....(SO) $	150.00-	175.00
#244..................set $	200.00-	250.00
#245 ....$	275.00-	325.00
#246 ....(PM) $	400.00-	500.00
#247 ....(PM/RD) $	2,200.00-	2,500.00
#248 ....(PM/RD) $	2,800.00-	3,200.00
#249 ....(PM/SD) $	1,000.00-	1,200.00
#250 ....(PM) $	600.00-	800.00
#251..................set $	600.00-	700.00
#252 ....(PM/SD) $	400.00-	500.00
#253 ....(PM) $	125.00-	150.00
#254 ....(PM) $	150.00-	175.00
#255 ....(PM) $	800.00-	1,000.00
#256 ....(SO) $	200.00-	250.00
#257 ....(PM) $	700.00-	800.00
#258..................set $	150.00-	200.00
#259 ....(SO) $	125.00-	175.00

#260 Chocolate Pot		
(PD) $	600.00-	700.00
Cup/Saucer ....$	100.00-	125.00
#261..........(PD/SO) $	150.00-	200.00
#262..........(PD/SO) $	125.00-	175.00
#263 ....$	225.00-	275.00
#264 ....$	50.00-	65.00
#265 ....(SM) $	50.00-	65.00
#266 ....$	225.00-	275.00
#267 ....$	300.00-	350.00
#268................(PD) $	100.00-	125.00
#269................(PD) $	225.00-	275.00
#270..........(PM/SF) $	275.00-	325.00
#271 ....$	300.00-	350.00
#272................(SD) $	150.00-	200.00
#273 ....$	600.00-	700.00
#274 ....$	600.00-	700.00
#275.........(PD) set $	550.00-	650.00
#276.........(RD/PM) $	500.00-	600.00
#277................(SO) $	225.00-	275.00
#278 Salt & Pepper		
(SO) ....set $	275.00-	325.00
TP...................$	200.00-	225.00
#279................(PD) $	700.00-	900.00
#280 ....$	100.00-	125.00
#281 ....(SO) set $	225.00-	275.00
#282................(SO) $	125.00-	150.00
#283................(SD) $	125.00-	150.00
#284................(SO) $	225.00-	275.00
#285 Chocolate Pot..$	600.00-	700.00
Cup/Saucer ....$	100.00-	125.00
#286 Demi-tasse Pot$	600.00-	700.00
Cup/Saucer $	100.00-	125.00
#287 Chocolate Pot..$	600.00-	700.00
Cup/Saucer .....$	100.00-	125.00
#288 Chocolate Pot..$	600.00-	700.00
Cup/Saucer .....$	100.00-	125.00
#289 ....(SO) set $	1,000.00-	1,200.00
#290 Cake Plate ......$	200.00-	250.00
Chocolate Pot..$	600.00-	700.00
Cup/Saucer .....$	100.00-	125.00
#291 ....(SD) set $	700.00-	900.00
#292 ....$	125.00-	150.00
#293................(SO) $	150.00-	200.00
#294 ....$	275.00-	325.00
#295..........(PD) set $	600.00-	800.00
#296 ....$	100.00-	125.00
#297................(RD) $	5,000.00-	6,000.00
#298 ....(SM) $	650.00-	750.00
#299 ....(PM/PD) $	750.00-	850.00
#300 ....(PM/PD) $	1,200.00-	1,400.00
#301..(PD/RM/RB) $	2,000.00-	2,200.00
#302.........(PD/RM) $	2,400.00-	2,600.00
#303 ....(PM) $	600.00-	700.00
#304..................set $	350.00-	450.00
#305 ....(PD) set $	225.00-	275.00
#306..................set $	200.00-	250.00
#307..................set $	200.00-	250.00
#308 ....(PM/SO) $	175.00-	225.00
#309 ....(SO) $	125.00-	150.00
#310 ....$	40.00-	60.00
#311 ....$	100.00-	125.00
#312..................set $	350.00-	450.00
#313 ....(SO) $	350.00-	400.00
#314..................set $	200.00-	250.00
#315..................set $	225.00-	275.00
#316 Coffee Pot ....$	600.00-	700.00
Cup/Saucer .....$	75.00-	100.00
C & S........set $	300.00-	350.00
#317 Coffee Pot ....$	600.00-	700.00
Cup/Saucer .....$	100.00-	125.00
#318 ....(PM) $	150.00-	175.00

#319 ....(PM) $	40.00-	60.00
#320 ....(PM/SD) $	450.00-	550.00
#321 ....(PM/SO) $	200.00-	225.00
#322..........(PM/SF) $	300.00-	350.00
#323 ....(PM) $	700.00-	800.00
#324 (SD/PM/SB)		
..................set $	1,600.00-	1,800.00
#325		
(SD/PM/SO) $	275.00-	325.00
#326		
(PD/PM/SB) $	1,400.00-	1,600.00
#327 ....(PM/SO) $	175.00-	225.00
#328 ....(PM) $	250.00-	300.00
#329 ....(PM) set $	350.00-	450.00
#330 ....(PM) $	550.00-	650.00
#331 ....(PM) $	600.00-	700.00
#332................(PD) $	300.00-	350.00
#333...................set $	200.00-	250.00
#334		
(SD/SM/SF) $	1,200.00-	1,400.00
#335................(SO) $	150.00-	200.00
#336 ....$	250.00-	300.00
#337 ....(PM/SO) $	225.00-	275.00
#338..........(PM/SF) $	800.00-	900.00
#339 ....(PM/PF) $	800.00-	900.00
#340 Chocolate Pot..$	800.00-	900.00
C & S Set ....$	300.00-	350.00
Cup/Saucer .....$	100.00-	125.00
Milk Pitcher....$	400.00-	500.00
#341 ....(PM/SO) $	250.00-	300.00
#342 ....(SO) $	225.00-	275.00
#343 ....(PM) $	250.00-	300.00
#344 ....(PM/SO) $	275.00-	325.00
#345		
(PD/PM/SO) $	300.00-	350.00
#346 ....(PM) $	125.00-	150.00
#347 ...(PD/PM) set $	1,200.00-	1,400.00
#348 ....$	550.00-	650.00
#349................(SO) $	200.00-	250.00
#350 ....$	600.00-	700.00
#351................(SO) $	300.00-	350.00
#352...................set $	200.00-	250.00
#353 ....$	150.00-	175.00
#354..........(PD/PF) $	300.00-	350.00
#355 Chocolate Pot..$	600.00-	700.00
Cup/Saucer .....$	100.00-	125.00
#356...................set $	225.00-	275.00
#357...................set $	150.00-	200.00
#358...................set $	175.00-	225.00
#359................(SD) $	125.00-	150.00
#360 ....$	350.00-	450.00
#361 ....$	300.00-	350.00
#362................(RD) $	5,500.00-	6,500.00
#363 ....(SM) $	550.00-	650.00
#364 ....(PM) $	600.00-	700.00
#365...................set $	225.00-	275.00
#366................(SO) $	250.00-	300.00
#367................(SO) $	225.00-	275.00
#368................(PD) $	300.00-	400.00
#369................(PD) $	250.00-	300.00
#370................(PD) $	225.00-	275.00
#371................(RD) $	500.00-	600.00
#372 ....(PM) $	225.00-	275.00
#373		
(SD/PM/PF) $	200.00-	275.00
#374 ....(SM) $	225.00-	275.00
#375 ....$	200.00-	250.00
#376................(RD) $	1,500.00-	1,800.00
#377 ....(SO) $	300.00-	400.00
#378 ....(SO) $	300.00-	400.00
#379 ....$	175.00-	225.00
#380 ....(PD/PM) $	225.00-	275.00

#381 ....$ 225.00- 275.00
#382 ....$ 200.00- 250.00
#383 ....(PD/PM) $ 250.00- 300.00
#384 ....$ 150.00- 200.00
#385 ....(PD/PM) $ 300.00- 400.00
#386 ....(PD) $ 150.00- 200.00
#387 ....(PM) $ 275.00- 325.00
#388 ....$ 75.00- 100.00
#389 ....$ 100.00- 125.00
#390 ....(RD) $ 800.00- 1,000.00
#391 ....$ 150.00- 200.00
#392 Tray...............$ 200.00- 250.00
Hair Receiver...$ 100.00- 150.00
Powder Box......$ 100.00- 150.00
#393 ....(RO) $ 600.00- 700.00
#394 ....(PD/RO) $ 500.00- 600.00
#395 ....(PM/SO) $ 175.00- 225.00
#396 ....(PM) $ 150.00- 200.00
#397 ....(RO) $ 400.00 500.00
#398 ....$ 150.00- 200.00
#399 ....(PM) $ 150.00- 200.00
#400 ....(SO/PF) $ 275.00- 325.00

#401 ....(PD/SO) $ 300.00- 350.00
#402 ....(SO) $ 250.00- 300.00
#403 ....
(RO w/liner) $ 350.00- 450.00
#404 ....(PD) $ 400.00- 500.00
#405 ....(PD) $ 400.00- 500.00
#406 ....(PD) $ 350.00- 450.00
#407 ....(RD/RO) $ 600.00- 700.00
#408 ....(PD) $ 500.00- 600.00
#409 ....(PD) $ 500.00- 600.00
#410 ....(SD) $ 1,200.00- 1,400.00
#411 ....(SD) $ 1,200.00- 1,400.00
#412 ....(SD) $ 1,200.00- 1,400.00
#413 ....(SD) $ 500.00- 600.00
#414 ....(SD) $ 300.00- 400.00
#415 ....$ 300.00- 400.00
#416 ....(PD/SM) $ 1,400.00- 1,600.00
#417 ....(SD) $ 1,000.00- 1,200.00
#418 ....(SD) $ 1,000.00- 1,200.00
#419 ....(SD) $ 1,000.00- 1,200.00
#420 ....(PD/RO) $ 600.00- 700.00
#421 ....(SD) $ 1,000.00- 1,200.00

#422 ....$ 350.00- 450.00
#423 ....(PF) $ 400.00- 500.00
#424 ....$ 400.00- 500.00
#425 ....$ 350.00- 450.00
#426 ....(PD) $ 800.00- 1,000.00
#427 ....(PD/PF) $ 1,400.00- 1,600.00
#428 ....(PD/SF) $ 1,400.00- 1,600.00
#429 ....
(PD/RM/SB) $ 2,200.00- 2,500.00
#430 ...(PD/RM/SB) $ 2,200.00- 2,500.00
#431 ....(SD) $ 1,000.00- 1,200.00
#432 ....
(PD/PM/SB) $ 1,400.00- 1,600.00
#433 ....(SF) 4 400.00- 500.00
#434 ....(SD/SF) $ 1,200.00- 1,400.00
#435 ....(PD) $ 800.00- 1,000.00
#436 ....(SD/RO) $ 800.00- 1,000.00
#437 ....
(PM/PF/SO) $ 1,000.00- 1,200.00

E. S. Germany (Erdmann Schlegelmilch) Prices for Photographs 438 to 524

#438 ....
(RMk/RM/RD) $ 1,000.00- 1,200.00
#439 ....
(RMk/RM/RF) $ 800.00- 900.00
#440 ....
(RMk/RM) $ 700.00- 800.00
#441 ....(RMk) $ 200.00- 250.00
#442 ....
(RMk/RM/RO) $ 700.00- 900.00
#443 ....$ 50.00- 75.00
#444 ....(SD) $ 75.00- 100.00
#445 Chocolate Pot..$ 200.00- 250.00
Cup/Saucer ....$ 40.00- 50.00
#446 ....(RO/PF) $ 300.00- 400.00
#447 ....(PD/PF) $ 300.00- 400.00
#448 ....(PD/PF) $ 250.00- 350.00
#449 ....(PD/PF) $ 250.00- 350.00
#450 ....(PD/SO) $ 75.00- 100.00
#451 ....(SD/SO) $ 175.00- 225.00
#452 ....(SO) $ 100.00- 125.00
#453 ....(SD/SO) $ 150.00- 200.00
#454 ....(SD/SB) $ 200.00- 250.00
#455 ....(SD) $ 75.00- 100.00
#456 ....(SD) $ 250.00- 350.00
#457 ....
(RM/PD/PF) $ 1,200.00- 1,400.00
#458 ....(SD/PF) $ 275.00- 325.00
#459 ....(PD/SM) $ 250.00- 300.00
#460 ....(PF/SM) $ 35.00- 45.00
#461 ....(PD/PF) $ 225.00- 275.00
#462 ....(PD/RF) $ 500.00- 600.00
#463 ....(PD/PF) $ 175.00- 225.00
#464 ....(PD/PF) $ 175.00- 225.00
#465 Tea Pot
(SD/PB) $ 250.00- 300.00
C & S.......set $ 200.00- 250.00
#466 ....(PD/PB) $ 50.00- 60.00

#467 ....(PD/PB) $ 150.00- 200.00
#468 ....(PD/PB) $ 50.00- 60.00
#469 ....(PD/SO) $ 200.00- 250.00
#470 ....(SD/PB) $ 150.00- 200.00
#471 ....(SD/PB) $ 800.00- 1,000.00
#472 ....(SD/PB) $ 400.00- 500.00
#473 ....(PD/PF) $ 400.00- 500.00
#474 ....(PD) $ 250.00- 350.00
#475 ....
(PD/RF/RO) $ 400.00- 500.00
#476 ....(PD/PF) $ 450.00- 550.00
#477 ....(PD/PF) $ 300.00- 400.00
#478 ....(PD/PF) $ 200.00- 300.00
#479 ....(PD/PB) $ 300.00- 400.00
#480 ....(PD/PF) $ 500.00- 600.00
#481 ....
(PD/PF/SM) $ 300.00- 400.00
#482 ....
(PD/PF/PB) $ 400.00- 500.00
#483 ....(PD/PF) $ 500.00- 600.00
#484 ....(PD) $ 500.00- 600.00
#485 ....(RD) $ 500.00- 600.00
#486 ....(RD) $ 800.00- 1,000.00
#487 ....(PD/PM) $ 500.00- 600.00
#488 ....(PD/PM) $ 500.00- 600.00
#489 ....(PD/RM) $ 1,000.00- 1,200.00
#490 ....
(PD/PF/RM) $ 800.00- 1,000.00
#491 ....(PD) $ 300.00- 400.00
#492 ....(PD) $ 300.00- 400.00
#493 ....
(PD/PF/RO) $ 600.00- 700.00
#494 ....(PD/RO) $ 800.00- 1,000.00
#495 ....(SD) $ 75.00- 100.00
#496 ....(SD) $ 75.00- 100.00
#497 ....pr. (SO) $ 250.00- 300.00
#498 ....(PF) $ 275.00- 325.00

#499 ....(RO) $ 400.00- 500.00
#500 ....$ 40.00- 60.00
#501 ....$ 40.00- 60.00
#502 ....$ 25.00- 35.00
#503 ....$ 25.00- 35.00
#504 ....$ 50.00- 65.00
#505 ....(PD) $ 350.00- 450.00
#506 Chocolate Pot..$ 175.00- 225.00
Cup/Saucer .....$ 30.00- 40.00
#507 ....(SO) $ 150.00- 200.00
#508 ....(SO) $ 125.00- 150.00
#509 .... (SO) set $ 800.00- 1,000.00
#510 ....$ 60.00- 75.00
#511 ....$ 30.00- 40.00
#512 ....$ 30.00- 40.00
#513 ....$ 30.00- 40.00
#514 ....(SMk) $ 40.00- 50.00
#515 ....pr.
(SO/SMk) $ 100.00- 125.00
#516 ....
(RO/SMk) $ 800.00- 1,000.00
#517 ....(SMk) set $ 100.00- 125.00
#518 ....(SMk) $ 100.00- 125.00
#519 ....(SMk) $ 40.00- 50.00
#520 ....(SMk) $ 40.00- 50.00
#521 ....(SMk) $ 40.00- 60.00
#522 ....
(SMk/SO) $ 125.00- 150.00
#523 ....(SMk) $ 25.00- 35.00
#524 ....(SMk) $ 50.00- 75.00

#525......(RMk)(ea) $	50.00-	75.00
#526............................		
(SO/RMk) $	175.00-	225.00
#527...............(SO) $	150.00-	200.00
#528...............(SO) $	125.00-	150.00
#529......................$	100.00-	125.00
#530...............(SM) $	75.00-	100.00
#531........(PM) set $	200.00-	250.00
#532...............(PM) $	125.00-	150.00
#533..........(RD/SF) $	1,000.00-	1,200.00
#534 ....(SD/SF) $	800.00-	1,000.00
#535...............(PB) $	250.00-	300.00
#536............................		
(SD/SM/PB) $	1,200.00-	1,400.00
#537..........(SD/PB) $	1,000.00-	1,200.00
#538..........(SO/PB) $	1,000.00-	1,200.00
#539......................$	550.00-	650.00
#540...............(SB) $	300.00-	350.00
#541...............(SB) $	300.00-	350.00
#542...............(PD) $	600.00-	800.00
#543......................$	100.00-	125.00
#544...............(PM) $	250.00-	300.00
#545......................$	125.00-	175.00
#546......................$	30.00-	40.00
#547...............(SO) $	125.00-	150.00
#548..........(SD/SO) $	225.00-	275.00
#549...............(RD) $	5,000.00-	7,000.00
#550...............(RD) $	5,000.00-	7,000.00
#551...............(SD) $	1,000.00-	1,200.00
#552............................		
(PD/SMk) $	1,000.00-	1,200.00
#553............................		
(SD/SMk) $	1,000.00-	1,200.00
#554............................		
(SD/SB/SMk) $	500.00-	700.00
#555............................		
(PD/PB/SMk) $	1,400.00-	1,600.00
#556............................		
(PD/SMk) $	500.00-	700.00
#557............................		
(RO/SMk) $	225.00-	275.00
#558............................		
(PD/SM/SMk) $	550.00-	650.00
#559............................		
(RO/SMk) $	450.00-	550.00
#560...............(SO) $	300.00-	400.00
#561......................$	200.00-	250.00
#562...............(PF) $	30.00-	45.00
#563...............(PF) $	30.00-	45.00
#564...............(PF) $	175.00-	225.00
#565...............(PM) $	225.00-	275.00
#566......................$	40.00-	50.00
#567...............(SM) $	50.00-	65.00
#568......................$	40.00-	50.00
#569......................$	20.00-	30.00
#570...............(SD) $	275.00-	325.00
#571...............(SD) $	250.00-	350.00
#572......................$	35.00-	50.00
#573......................$	45.00-	60.00
#574......................$	45.00-	60.00

#575......................$	25.00-	40.00
#576...............(SD) $	350.00-	450.00
#577...............(SD) $	$150.00-	200.00
#578...............(SD) $	350.00-	450.00
#579...............(SD) $	350.00-	450.00
#580......................$	30.00-	45.00
#581......................$	50.00-	65.00
#582......................$	50.00-	65.00
#583......................$	45.00-	60.00
#584......................$	35.00-	45.00
#585......................$	15.00-	20.00
#586...............(SD) $	30.00-	45.00
#587...............(SD) $	$50.00-	75.00
#588 Chocolate Pot..$	100.00-	150.00
Cup/Saucer .....$	25.00-	35.00
#589 Chocolate Pot..$	250.00-	300.00
Cup/Saucer .....$	40.00-	50.00
#590 Coffee Pot ......$	225.00-	275.00
C & S........set $	150.00-	200.00
Tray.......(SO) $	125.00-	150.00
#591 Chocolate Pot..$	250.00-	300.00
Cup/Saucer .....$	40.00-	50.00
#592...............(RO) $	250.00-	350.00
#593......................$	200.00-	250.00
#594......................$	200.00-	250.00
#595 Chocolat Pot ...$	100.00-	125.00
Coffee Pot ......$	200.00-	250.00
#596......................$	100.00-	125.00
#597...............(PD) $	40.00-	60.00
#598......................$	125.00-	150.00
#599...............(PM)		
Chocolate Pot..$	600.00-	700.00
Cup/Saucer .....$	100.00-	125.00
#600...............(RO) $	175.00-	225.00
#601......................$	25.00-	40.00
#602......................$	30.00-	45.00
#603......................$	200.00-	250.00
#604...............(SO) $	150.00-	200.00
#605...............(SO) $	150.00-	200.00
#606...............(SO)		
Salt & Pepper		
set...................$	125.00-	150.00
Cruet .....(RO) $	125.00-	150.00
#607...............(SO)		
Salt & Pepper		
set...................$	125.00-	150.00
Mustard ....$	100.00-	125.00
Tray ....$	60.00	75.00
#608......................$	35.00-	50.00
#609......................$	75.00-	100.00
#610...............(SO) $	100.00-	125.00
#611...................set $	$50.00-	75.00
#612...................set $	75.00-	100.00
#613...............(SD) $	125.00-	150.00
#614...............(RO) $	125.00-	150.00
#615..........(SO/PF) $	150.00-	175.00
#616......................$	40.00-	50.00
#617...............(SO) $	175.00-	225.00
#618...............(SO) $	30.00-	40.00
#619...(PD/PM/SO) $	125.00-	175.00

#620...............set $	250.00-	300.00
#621...............(SO) $	100.00-	125.00
#622 Tray...............$	75.00-	100.00
CH pair ....$	125.00-	150.00
Cov. Boxes ea..$	50.00-	65.00
#623 Tray...............$	125.00-	150.00
HR ....$	50.00-	75.00
PB ....$	50.00-	75.00
#624...............(SO) $	100.00-	125.00
#625......................$	40.00-	50.00
#626......................$	25.00-	35.00
#627.........(PD/RO) $	400.00-	500.00
#628............................		
(SD/PM/RO) $	600.00-	800.00
#629...............(SO) $	150.00-	175.00
#630...............(PD) $	200.00-	250.00
#631...............(SD) $	75.00-	100.00
#632..........(SD/SB) $	800.00-	1,000.00
#633 CP ....$	100.00-	125.00
Cup/Saucer .....$	50.00-	65.00
Syrup ....$	175.00-	225.00
Gravy ....$	60.00-	75.00
Celery..............$	60.00-	75.00
#634......................$	50.00-	75.00
#635...............(SO) $	100.00-	150.00
#636......................$	30.00-	40.00
#637......................$	25.00-	40.00
#638........................		
(PM/SMk) $	100.00-	125.00
#639............................		
(PM/SMk) $	75.00-	100.00
#640............................		
(SD/SMk) $	100.00-	125.00
#641........(PD/SMk)		
Chamberstick .$	200.00-	250.00
Tray...............$	600.00-	800.00
HP ....$	250.00-	275.00
Pin box ea. ......$	100.00-	125.00
#642............................		
(RO/PF/SMk) $	400.00-	500.00
#643............................		
(PD/RO/SMk) $	700.00-	800.00
#644............................		
(SD/SMk) $	1,000.00-	1,200.00
#645............................		
(SD/SMk) $	800.00-	1,000.00
#646............................		
(RD/SMk) $	1,200.00-	1,400.00
#647............................		
(SD/RO/SMk) $	800.00-	1,000.00
#648.........(SMk) pr. $	400.00-	600.00
#649 ....(SMk) $	225.00-	275.00
#650......................$	125.00-	150.00
#651......................$	125.00-	150.00
#652......................$	30.00-	45.00
#653......................$	35.00-	50.00
#654..........(RO) pr. $	400.00-	600.00
#655......................$	60.00-	80.00
#656......................$	50.00-	65.00

O. S. (Oscar Schlegelmilch)
Prices for Photographs 657 to 674

#620 .... set $	250.00-	300.00	#663			#671		
#657 ....(PF/SMk) $	350.00-	400.00	(SD/PB/SMk) $	550.00-	650.00	(PD/SO/SMk) $	400.00-	500.00
#658			#664 ....(SD/SMk) $	400.00-	500.00	#672		
(PD/PB/SMk) $	400.00-	450.00	#665 ....(PD/SMk) $	150.00	200.00	(SD/SO/SMk) $	700.00-	800.00
#659			#666			#673		
(PD/PB/SMk) $	400.00-	450.00	(SO/SMk) set $	250.00-	300.00	(SD/PB/SMk) $	400.00-	500.00
#660			#667 ....(SMk) $	200.00-	250.00	#674		
(PD/PB/SMk) $	450.00-	500.00	#668 ....(SD/SMk) $	400.00-	500.00	(SD/PB/SMk) set $	700.00-	900.00
#661			#669					
(PD/PB/SMk) $	400.00-	500.00	(PD/PB/SMk) $	750.00	850.00			
#662			#670					
(PD/PB/SMk) $	175.00-	225.00	(PD/SMk) $	300.00-	400.00			

Other Books by Mary Frank Gaston

The Collector's Encyclopedia of Limoges Porcelain II $19.95
The Collector's Encyclopedia of R.S. Prussia $24.95
The Collector's Encyclopedia of Flow Blue China $19.95
Blue Willow ....$ 9.95
American Belleek $19.95
Art Deco $14.95
Antique Brass and Copper $16.95

These titles may be ordered from the author or the publisher.
Include $2.00 for the first book, 30¢ for each additional book ordered.

Mary Frank Gaston
P.O. Box 342
Bryan, TX 77806

Collector Books
P.O. Box 3009
Paducah, KY 42002

Schroeder's Antiques Price Guide

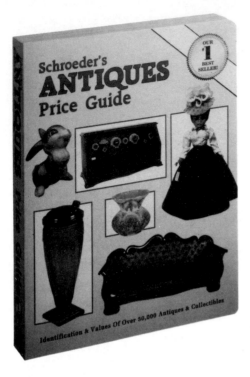

Schroeder's Antiques Price Guide has become THE household name in the antiques & collectibles field. Our team of editors works year-round with more than 200 contributors to bring you our #1 best-selling book on antiques & collectibles.

With more than 50,000 items identified & priced, Schroeder's is a must for the collector & dealer alike. If it merits the interest of today's collector, you'll find it in Schroeder's. Each subject is represented with histories and background information. In addition, hundreds of sharp original photos are used each year to illustrate not only the rare and unusual, but the everyday "fun-type" collectibles as well — not postage stamp pictures, but large close-up shots that show important details clearly.

Our editors compile a new book each year. Never do we merely change prices. Accuracy is our primary aim. Prices are gathered over the entire year previous to publication, from ads and personal contacts. Then each category is thoroughly checked to spot inconsistencies, listings that may not be entirely reflective of actual market dealings, and lines too vague to be of merit. Only the best of the lot remains for publication. You'll find Schroeder's Antiques Price Guide the one to buy for factual information and quality.

No dealer, collector or investor can afford not to own this book. It is available from your favorite bookseller or antiques dealer at the low price of $12.95. If you are unable to find this price guide in your area, it's available from Collector Books, P.O. Box 3009, Paducah, KY 42002-3009 at $12.95 plus $2.00 for postage and handling.

8½ x 11", 608 Pages   **$12.95**

COLLECTOR BOOKS
A Division of Schroeder Publishing Co., Inc.